Edward Pollock, Selden C. Judson

Sketch book of Lynchburg, Va

Its people and its trade

Edward Pollock, Selden C. Judson

Sketch book of Lynchburg, Va
Its people and its trade

ISBN/EAN: 9783744735643

Printed in Europe, USA, Canada, Australia, Japan

Cover: Foto ©Suzi / pixelio.de

More available books at **www.hansebooks.com**

PEOPLE AND ITS TRADE.

ILLUSTRATED.

PUBLISHED BY
EDWARD POLLOCK AND S. C. JUDSON.

EDWARD POLLOCK, COMPILER AND EDITOR.

LYNCHBURG, VA.:
PRINTED BY THE VIRGINIAN JOB PRINTING HOUSE,
1887.

GENERAL VIEW OF LYNCHBURG FROM AMHERST HEIGHTS.

LYNCHBURG.

1887.

DESCRIPTIVE.

INTRODUCTORY.

LYNCHBURG, the principal inland City of Virginia, lies on the northern boundary of Campbell County, being situated on the south bank of the James River, about one hundred and twenty miles above the head of tide-water navigation at Richmond, and two hundred and fifty miles above the point at which this noble and majestic stream empties its waters into Hampton Roads, at the mouth of Chesapeake Bay. The City is exactly midway between the magnificent harbor of Norfolk and Portsmouth—unequalled on the Atlantic seaboard—and the Tennessee boundary line at Bristol, from each of which points it is distant two hundred and four miles by the Norfolk & Western Railroad.

Like the Eternal City, Lynchburg stands upon seven hills, which give it a highly picturesque appearance, besides affording it abundant facilities for perfect drainage. From the bold and irregular character of its foundations it derives its *sobriquet*, "The Hill City." It is also known as "The Tobacco City," from the fact of its central position in the district chiefly devoted to the production of the best grades of this "bewitching vegetable," which forms its principal article of commerce and manufacture. It is copiously supplied with water by large reservoirs, as well as by numerous bold springs. Pure soft water is also easily procurable by wells of moderate depth. The City is lighted throughout by electricity, and the "Gamewell" Fire Alarm and Southern Bell Telephone systems are in use. The principal streets are well paved with granite blocks, and a line of street cars almost encircles the business portion of the City, and extends a mile beyond its southwestern limits, to the Fair Grounds. This line is now being lengthened, and, when finished, will form a complete circuit, passing within easy reach of all the principal thoroughfares in the City and suburbs.

The numerous handsome factories and stores, mills and warehouses, churches and public buildings, give to the City a business-like and substantial aspect, while the many graceful residences which crown the hills and adorn the numberless eligible sites in the City and its suburbs, bespeak alike the wealth and refined taste of the population generally.

SCENERY.

The surroundings of Lynchburg are peculiarly romantic and beautiful. To the South and East, far as the eye can reach, the landscape may be described as irregularly undulating, varied here and there by gently sloping hills and fertile vales, and relieved by an occasional remnant of primeval forest. On the Northeast, the view is bounded by the bluffs or "Heights" of the neighboring County of Amherst, past whose feet the broad and rapid James, spanned at and near this point by several dams and bridges, hastens with its message of greeting from the mountains to the sea. To the northward, at a distance of about twenty miles to their base, the Blue Ridge Mountains rise in gentle grandeur and in varying height, visible, in clear weather, for seventy-five miles along the range, and culminating, at their southwestern extremity, in the far-famed Peaks of Otter, towering skyward in their matchless stateliness and symmetry.

INDUSTRIAL ADVANTAGES.

The geographical position of the City is such as to give it extraordinary manufacturing and commercial advantages. Three great railroad lines, having connections which afford easy and direct access to every section of the United States, intersect here; while other roads, of a more local character, will shortly make this their terminus.

With a water power capable of meeting any possible requirement, the City offers special inducements to the investment of brains and capital in various kinds of industrial enterprise.

The development of the vast mineral wealth of the neighboring territory is as yet in its infancy, but it is already known to be practically inexhaustible. Coal of the best quality is also abundant and cheap, while the products of the farm and forest are rich, plentiful and varied.

CLIMATE.

The topography of the City and surrounding country, its elevation above the sea—over 500 feet on the river bank—and the purity of its atmosphere, make this climate singularly healthy, and especially beneficial to invalids. There are no marshes or stagnant pools, and the neighborhood is entirely free from malarial disorders. The winters are short and mild, seldom of more than three months' duration, and are generally dry and pleasant. Snow seldom lies here longer than a few days, and there is but little interruption to agricultural pursuits during the entire winter. The heat of summer, which is never extreme, is tempered by the delicious southwest breezes and the cool sweet air from the neighboring mountains. The nights are always balmy and refreshing, and the days rarely oppressive.

During the summer months, near the eastern base of the Blue Ridge Mountains, there are more frequent showers than in any other part of Virginia. The explanation of this is to be found in the fact that the prevailing wind at that season comes direct from the sea, and its moisture, when driven against the mountain barrier, meets with a colder stratum of air and becomes condensed, thus producing the welcome showers which refresh and invigorate the growing crops, while in less favored sections the ground remains parched and dry.

The mean temperature of Piedmont Virginia, which, as its name implies, lies at the foot of the Blue Ridge Mountains, and near the centre of which the City of Lynchburg is situated, is stated by Col. Randolph Harrison, Commissioner of Agriculture, in his *Hand Book of Virginia*, published last year (1886), to be as follows: annual, 53.7; winter, 44; summer, 78; while the rainfall is placed at "32 to 44 inches." In reference to this Division of the State, Col. Harrison writes: "For beauty of landscape, variety of scenery, native fertility of soil, water courses contributing to practical benefit as well as to beauty of scenery, this section is surpassed by few, if any, other sections in the United States."

And Dr. Ellzey, of Washington, D. C., in an *Address before the*

Southern Association, says: "In its physical features, picturesque and lovely to an unusual degree: in climate, temperate and healthful, in the abundance and variety of its productions, unsurpassed; in all that makes life desirable and home what it should be, there is no place in this world which surpasses Piedmont Virginia—there are very few which come near it."

AGRICULTURE.

The greater part of Campbell County, however, belongs, from a geological standpoint, to that one of the "Grand Divisions" of the State known as "Middle Virginia;" and of this Col. Harrison writes, as follows:

"Here is the great tobacco region of Virginia—the lands of the upper and lower jurassic period or new red sandstone being especially adapted to the finer qualities. The formation is identical with that of Lancaster County, Pa. and the lower Connecticut Valley, where the cultivation of seed leaf tobacco has enriched the community to an almost incredible degree.

* * * * * *

"Middle Virginia is an undulating country—hills, table-lands and intervales—living springs and never-failing water courses everywhere. The soils vary greatly—the bottom-lands generally very fertile, and the up-lands are often very productive, especially when the rocks contain epidote and some varieties of horn blende.

* * * * *

"The productions of this region are varied. Tobacco has been mentioned as the staple of a large part of this Division of the State, but its cultivation is by no means universal—in many counties it is not grown at all. Everywhere the cereals and fruits of temperate climates, notably the apple and grape, grow in perfection; and while we have not yet reached the grazing sections proper, we find clover, timothy, orchard and other grasses growing here and there in great luxuriance; and they show a natural adaptation to grass, which, however, so far from having been encouraged, has persistently been thwarted—fought against—from the first settlement of the country until recently. 'Killing grass' has been the object kept steadily in view in growing tobacco and Indian corn, and, with the large force of slaves inhabiting this region, was so effectually done, that it came to be believed by many that the valuable forage and pasture grasses would not grow here, despite the fact that 'blue grass'—poa compressa (the true 'blue grass')—the identical grass which is so highly valued in Fauquier and Loudoun for making fat pastures—is the grass which has given the planters most trouble to keep under; which has made such a struggle for existence that it has never been extirpated in this region ; but, where it has half an opportunity, will assert its rights and will take possession of the land, crowding out wheat, or whatever may, at the time, be in occupancy.

"Clover has long been successfully grown here; and the idea that timothy, orchard, etc., would not succeed, has been disproved by the logic of facts. There is scarcely a county in this region in which there are not meadows that would compare favorably with the best anywhere; few though they be, they demonstrate the possibility. The

SIXTH STREET BRIDGE AND UNION DEPOT.
(FROM BLACKWATER CREEK.)

renovation of this healthful and most improvable region will be brought about by clothing a large portion of the country with meadow and pasture grasses."

FOREST GROWTH.

"The 'Sylva' gradually changes as we ascend from the Tidewater Division to Piedmont. The cypress disappears, the long-leaf pine ceases to grow after the first tier of counties is passed, and the cedar and holly, the gum and willow oak, become more and more infrequent. The short-leaf, or hard yellow pine, furnishes its valuable timber in every part of Middle Virginia, but does not take exclusive possession of large tracts of land as in Tidewater, except where it is found as 'second growth' on lands which have been cultivated and then turned out to grow up again. There it takes the place of the genuine 'lob-lolly,' or old field pine of Tidewater—the long-leaf variety—the 'pinus taeda' of botanists. In the forests of Middle Virginia the pine (short-leaf, yellow and two other varieties too rare to deserve a description) grows along with the various oaks, the tulip tree, hickory, walnut, locust, maple, ash and other timber of minor importance; and, on the streams, sycamore, beech, birch, willow and maple. At some distance from the mountains we again find chestnut in large quantities. In fine, the forest growth of this section is of singular variety, beauty and value."

MINERALS.

"The mineral resources of this region are very great. Besides the coal of the mesozoic areas of Richmond and Farmville, this country yields gold, silver, copper and iron ores in great variety and abundance, and, for architectural purposes, fine gray granite, gneiss, and brown stone, Potomac or brecciated marble, and the finest slate for roofing purposes; also mica, kaolin and asbestos and limestone.

* * * * * *

"The veins of iron ore are numerous, some of the magnetic ores having a thickness of four feet; the beds of hematite ore, particularly those upon either border of the belt, as along James river, where it runs parallel with it, and in the 'Wilderness,' near the Rappahannock, are very thick and extensive. The first successful furnaces in America, those of the colonial Governor Spotswood, were supplied from the latter beds.

"There are also large beds of this ore where the Chesapeake and Ohio railway crosses the belt. In this vicinity the valuable sulphurets of iron and copper are found, and there will soon be large sulphuric acid works and a manufactory of fertilizers here, turning out copper and iron as by-products.

"The slates of the middle country are excellent for all purposes, notably those of Buckingham and Amherst counties. In Buckingham they have been long and extensively quarried for roofing, flagging, mantles, &c. The sandstone of the imposed 'middle secondary' are valuable for building purposes, as are also the 'brownstones' of the red sandstone, which are extensively quarried at Manassas. The infusorial earth, so abundant in Richmond, is valuable as a polishing material."

RAILROADS.

"This country is favored in respect of means of transportation, railroads penetrating it in every direction The great 'Coast Line,' which passes through the State from Washington to Weldon close to the divide between Middle Virginia and Tidewater, almost on the line between the archæan and the tertiary formations—sometimes in one and sometimes in the other—belongs equally to both. From Washington and Alexandria ray out the Washington, Ohio & Western, and the Virginia Midland, with its various branches; from Fredericksburg, the narrow gauge to Orange C. H.; from Richmond, the Chesapeake & Ohio stretches out through Henrico, Hanover and Louisa into Piedmont, and thence to the Ohio and beyond; and the Alleghany, along the beautiful valley of James River through Middle Virginia into Piedmont and Appalachia. The Richmond & Danville road penetrates this part of Virginia for a hundred and fifty miles before passing into North Carolina, and sends out a branch at Keysville and another at Sutherlin. The Brighthope road from Bermuda Hundred taps the coal region at Clover Hill, twenty-odd miles away. At Petersburg, the Norfolk & Western road passes from Tidewater into Middle Virginia, and, after a course of more than a hundred and twenty miles in this Division, strikes out Southwest through Piedmont and the Valley to the Tennessee line at Bristol. The Atlantic & Danville is in course of construction from the point to which it is now completed, Hicksford, in Greensville County, to Danville and beyond; and the Southern link of the Virginia Midland extends from Lynchburg to Danville, with a branch from Elba Station into Franklin county. All these roads intersect this Division of Virginia, and there are others projected, and probably soon to be built."

HYGIENE.

"Except in limited localities, in and near certain water courses, where malarial diseases prevail to some extent, this is an exceptionally healthy region, perhaps as favorable to longevity as any part of America—we might almost say, *of the world.*"

To this official statement may be added the singular and important fact that on no single occasion has infectious or contagious disease of any kind ever gained a foothold or assumed an epidemic form in the City of Lynchburg. Sporadic cases have of course appeared, from time to time, but they have never been known to spread here. Indeed it would seem that the climate of this favored region is fatal to nothing save only disease and pestilence, while to all else its effects are eminently stimulating and wholesome.

THE BLUE RIDGE REGION.

As Lynchburg lies within twenty miles of the base of the Blue Ridge Mountains proper, and upon the plateau known as the "sub range" at an average elevation of 700 feet, or thereabouts, above the tidewater level, the following information with regard to the sanatory properties of this climate will doubtless prove of interest to the reader

Major Jed. Hotchkiss, in *The Virginias*, June, 1884, says:

"We would call attention to the fact that the Blue Ridge region in Virginia is, as can be proven by the testimony of consumptives fully restored to health, the best *Sanitarium* in the United States east of the Mississippi. The sheltered eastern slopes of the long stretch of that mountain range in Virginia, above the line of 1,000 feet of elevation above the ocean level and under that of 2,500, offers hundreds of localities for health resorts for people afflicted with pulmonary diseases, that surpass any other that we know of or have read of. During the past thirty-six years the writer has frequently recommended this region to persons having such diseases, and in every case where the advice was followed, a restoration to health has resulted. If any one is sceptical about the efficacy of the Blue Ridge air, water and exercises, as remedial agents for lung troubles, let him spend a few months at some point in this belt, and we will make him the referee to sustain the opinion here advanced. A young man from Vermont, a victim of this especially fearful New England disease, took his advice and spent the winter of 1882-83 there, and went away with restored health that still continues. We could name other cases.

"About the best such people could do would be to buy a few acres of the Sunward dry air slope of the Blue Ridge in Virginia, and busy themselves raising grapes and other fruits while inhaling health and strength. There are at least 200,000 acres of such sanitary country for occupation, room for 20,000 people with ten acres for each, and none of it remote from railways or markets; and here, too, is the region for building up extensive establishments for health and pleasure that will have a large all-the-year-round patronage."

General McDonald, editor of the *Industrial South*, referring to the above, says:

"We may say that we have some personal knowledge of the particular locality mentioned, and from our own observation are quite inclined to acquiesce in the opinion of Major Hotchkiss. Among others whom we met at Afton (in this belt) was a very intelligent and pleasant gentleman in the government service at Washington, from whom we learned that, being subject to rhuematism, he thought it well, before determining where he would spend his summer vacation, to consult the Signal Bureau—the desideratum being a dry atmosphere. The officers examined their records, and reported to him that the dryest mountain atmosphere of which they had knowledge was at a place on the Blue Ridge called Afton—of which he had never before heard—and his experience had attested the correctness of the advice that sent him there. So dry is the atmosphere that a newspaper spread on the grass at night shows no sign of moisture next morning, although the night is much cooler than the day."

PUBLIC IMPROVEMENTS.

The reports of the Standing Committees of the City Council for

FIREMEN'S MEMORIAL FOUNTAIN.
(ON CHURCH STREET, AT FOOT OF COURT HOUSE HILL.)

the fiscal years ending February 1st, 1884, 1885, 1886 and 1887, respectively, furnish some very interesting matter relative to the various departments of the Municipal Government. It will be seen at a glance that the City Fathers are fully alive to the wisdom, if not the necessity, of a liberal and progressive policy as regards public improvements of all kinds, while a closer examination will disclose the fact that the bonded debt of the City—always within the limits permitted by the charter—has increased but little, comparatively speaking, despite the large outlay necessitated by the grand results.

The following is from the Report of the Finance Committee for the year ending February 1st, 1884:

"The Water Works, with its ponderous machinery, lifting water 350 feet, has supplied the whole City with water. The truss, conveying water across Blackwater Creek, was erected at great cost, and your Reservoir on Clay Street stands as sponsor for $50,000 well spent.

"Then, too, you no longer wait for the application of human muscle to the Court House bell to give the alarm of that dreaded element, fire. Electricity holds the hammer in check, ever ready to respond to a simple touch given to a wire in any quarter of the City. You have, in a word, organized (through the zeal and public spirit of the able gentlemen composing the Board of Fire Commissioners) a Department second to that of no city in America. You have improved your public buildings, adding to some here and erecting new ones there—notably your fire stations and improvement to the Court House, Jail and Alms House. The avenues of approach to the City have not been neglected, as can be seen by a passing glance at Grace Street and its continuation; Cabell Street, too, and then others still in contemplation. The sewers of the City, too, have not been overlooked; much money not appropriated in the annual ordinance was expended for sewerage, in order to preserve the health of your constituents. So far, then, have you gone in the way of public improvements, and there is, so far as your Committee is advised, but one verdict; certainly there is no complaint because it has been done. It is true some adverse criticism attended the organization of the Fire Department and the construction of the fire alarm telegraph. Subsequent events have hushed this, and the wisdom of your action can no longer be questioned.

* * * *

"Your Charter permits you to issue bonds to an amount equal to eighteen per cent. of the real and personal property—taxable values—of the City. In comparing your debt with that of other Virginia cities of last year, we find—

The debt of		Alexandria	was	23	per cent.	of	its taxable	values.
"	"	Danville	"	19	"	"	"	"
"	"	Norfolk	"	17	"	"	"	"
"	"	Petersburg	"	12½	"	"	"	"
"	"	Richmond	"	12	"	"	"	"
"	"	Lynchburg	"	11	"	"	"	"

* * * * * * *

"It is proper to state that the City has not a dollar of floating debt."

From the Report of the City Engineer:

"Within a few past years a wonderful change has been wrought in the character and efficiency of the water works; a new pump house has been erected, three powerful water engines are in position, a new reservoir nearly completed, and the distributive pipe system extended in different directions—probably a little beyond the limit of a prudential consideration. An appreciative public has not failed to commend such successful efforts, and will continue to do so as long as we can revel in the enjoyment of an abundant water supply for domestic purposes, for gushing fountains, and other privileges, even the use of water for motive power.

* * * * * *

RUINS OF THE OLD QUAKER MEETING HOUSE.
(ON SALEM TURNPIKE.)

"The Street Department has exhibited remarkable activity during the past year, and more permanent works have been executed than during any preceding year since the incorporation of the City."

From the Report of the Committee on Water:

"The Committee has the most gratifying announcement to make to the City Council that the water has not been turned off the city for a single hour during the past year. Occasional repairs in different sections of the corporation have caused a suspension, for a few hours, of the supply, but the quantity in storage has been ample for all the needs of the consumers for nearly two years, or since March 3, 1882."

JOSEPH COHN,

LYNCHBURG'S LEADING AND ONLY

One-Price Clothier, Tailor, Furnisher and Hatter.

IMPRESS THESE FACTS ON YOUR MIND:

I offer you the Largest Stock in the State to select from.

I name the Lowest Prices, and have but One-Price for Everybody.

Specialist in Fine Clothing for Men, Youths, Boys and Children.

Sole agent for this city of Knox' World-Renowned Derby and Silk Hats.

824, 826 and 828 Main Street,

From the Report of the Committee on Fire:

"An entire reorganization of the Fire Department has taken place during the last twelve months, and instead of a volunteer, a paid organization has been established, and the cost of maintaining the latter has increased immensely; but the greater efficiency is thought to be commensurate with the expense. March the 16, 1883, an ordinance was passed, appointing three Fire Commissioners, one from each ward, whose duty it was to organize a paid department; and the

MR. JOSEPH COHN'S CLOTHING ESTABLISHMENT.
(CORNER OF MAIN AND NINTH STREETS.)

manner and means adopted by that Commission, and the abundant success which has crowned its efforts, has been attested by all who passed through the trying ordeal of last Fall, when there seemed to be a systematic attempt to burn the City. Every night, and frequently twice in one night, fires were kindled by the hands of an incendiary. All praise is due the new Department for preventing immense loss of property and probable loss of life in that awful emergency."

From the Chief Engineer of the Fire Department:

"Since the organization of this force, the Gamewell Fire Alarm System has been introduced. * * * *

"To say that this system of alarm has proven very satisfactory, and, so far as its jurisdiction extends, is a complete success, I pay but a small tribute to its inestimable worth and pre-eminence over all other methods, indicating, as it does instantly, the location, or thereabouts, of a fire, thereby enabling the Department to repair to it immediately. It has been the means of saving much property."

From the Report of the Committee on Schools:

"It is gratifying to your Committee to be able to report that the Public Schools of the city are in a prosperous and improved condition.

"The increase in the number of pupils attending during the last scholastic year was great—much greater than the increase in the school population of the city. The attendance was more regular and prompt, and the standard of scholarship higher than in any previous year."

From the Report of the Committee on Police:

"Your Committee takes pleasure in again testifying to the admirable management of the Board of Police Commissioners. The City was never better served than it has been during the period under review, and consequently your Committee has no recommendations to offer for the coming year."

In the Reports for the year ending February 1st, 1885, appear the following:

From the Committee on Sewers:

"The first annual report of your Committee on Sewers is presented under circumstances, as we conceive, of considerable encouragement. Only one year has elapsed since the organization of this Department, during which time the results of its operations will compare favorably with similar work executed during any preceding year, when this branch of the public work was combined with the Street Department.

"Over 2,200 yards, or 1¼ miles, of terra cotta pipes have been laid in various places. The Eighth Street culvert has been extended 140 feet, and the old sewers have been repaired wherever necessary."

From the Chief Engineer of the Fire Department:

"In submitting this, my second Annual Report of the operations and progress of this Department for the past year, it is with much pleasure, not unmingled with pride, that I point to our Fire Record, showing, as it does, the very small loss within its fire limits of $5,-156,30.

"Our city may well feel proud of its superb water supply. Even during the past summer, when cities over the entire Union were clamoring for water, our reservoirs never failed, an abundance was to

BIRD'S-EYE VIEW OF LYNCHBURG, FROM WHITE ROCK.

be had during the whole time, and effective streams were obtainable from all plugs without the use of engine, except those on level with the highest reservoir."

From the Committee on Schools:

"We are pleased to be able to report that your Public Schools have never been in a more prosperous condition. There has been a great

F. C. BROWN,

1314, 1316, 1318, 1320 Jefferson St.,

LYNCHBURG, - VIRGINIA.

(ESTABLISHED IN 1815.)

THE OLDEST BUSINESS HOUSE IN THE CITY.

J. H. C. WINSTON, SON & McGEHEE,

(Successor to E. J. Folkes and Folkes & Winston.)

620 and 622 Main Street,
LYNCHBURG, - VIRGINIA,

MANUFACTURERS OF AND DEALERS IN

FURNITURE, MATTRESSES, AND CHAIRS OF ALL KINDS.

WE ALWAYS KEEP ON HAND A LINE OF

FINE PARLOR AND CHAMBER SUITS, SIDEBOARDS AND EXTENSION TABLES, AND FINE FANCY TABLES AND PEDESTALS, LADIES' DESK AND PARLOR CABINETS, IN WALNUT, MAHOGANY AND ANTIQUE OAK.

Our prices cannot be beaten, and it will pay you to call and examine our stock before purchasing elsewhere.

increase in attendance within the last year; a steady improvement in the system of instruction and the average standard of scholarship attained by the pupils. At a Convention of all the City and County School Superintendents of the State, just held in Richmond, our schools have taken nearly all the first medals and certificates of distinction awarded for excellence."

From the Committee on Police:

"Since our last annual report there have been no changes whatever in the administration of the Police Department. The service has been thoroughly efficient and satisfactory, and no recommendations are considered necessary."

From the Mayor's Message to the City Council:

"The energy, ability and courage shown by the gentlemen composing the Board of Fire Commissioners in dealing with the tremendous problem thrust upon the community by the total collapse of the volunteer Fire Department, should ever be gratefully remembered by our people. The efficiency of the department organized by them is shown by the statement of the chief that the loss from fires to which the Department responded during the last year, both within and without the fire limits, was only $27,382.50, whilst the property saved was valued at $72,628.70.

"The determination of the gentlemen composing this board, as well as the Board of Police Commissioners, to allow none but first-rate men to remain on the force under their control, has been ably seconded by the chiefs of these departments and has resulted in giving us a body of policemen and firemen who will compare favorably with those of any city. I have found the members of the police force sober, faithful, active and vigilant; the officers and many of the men well acquainted with the ordinances of the city, whilst the chief has been indefatigable in his efforts to promote the discipline and efficiency of his force, and to preserve the peace and good order of the community. The Board of Police Commissioners have never hesitated to remove any man who impaired the efficiency of the force; have administred the trust committed to their charge with the strictest economy, and, in all matters, have been actuated by an earnest desire for the public welfare.

"Our public schools are now, as they have been ever since their organization, among the best in the State. The names composing the list of teachers are a sufficient guaranty that they enjoy, as they richly deserve to, the confidence of the community.

* * * * * *

"In conclusion, I think the condition of our community is highly gratifying; the depression in business has been less severely felt here than in most places, and is now passing away; your furnaces, work-

DRUGS AND MEDICINES

— AT —

WHOLESALE AND RETAIL.

We are occupying our MAGNIFICENT NEW HOUSE, ON THE CORNER OF MAIN AND TENTH STREETS, and have the largest and handsomest Drug Establishment in Virginia. There are few larger, and our Retail Room (25x132 feet) is unquestionably the HANDSOMEST in the Southern States. (See cut on opposite page.)

We are adding daily to our already large stock, and OUR FACILITIES ARE EQUAL TO ANY, for satisfying our friends and customers.

OUR WHOLESALE AND RETAIL DEPARTMENTS

comprise everything usually found in a FIRST-CLASS CITY DRUG ESTABLISHMENT. We make a SPECIALTY of selling to Country Stores, and GUARANTEE SATISFACTION in every particular.

OUR PROPRIETARY MEDICINES

some of which are sold all over the United States, are EQUAL TO ANY MADE, and pay better profits than other similar goods. Orders are filled with promptness always.

☞ A TRIAL ORDER is respectfully solicited, by mail or otherwise, and we will be glad to have our friends call to see us, whether they buy or not.

FAULKNER & CRAIGHILL,

Wholesale Druggists, Manufacturers and Proprietors of Camm's Emulsion,

1000 MAIN STREET, LYNCHBURG, VA.

JOHN J. MALLAN & BRO.,

—DEALERS IN—

Family Groceries, Dry Goods, Notions, Wines, Liquors, &c.

604 MAIN STREET,

LYNCHBURG, - VIRGINIA.

MALLAN BROTHERS,

—DEALERS IN—

Coal, Wood, Baled Forage, Mill Feed, Corn, Hay, Oats,

Bran, Lime, &c.,

714 FIFTH AVENUE, - LYNCHBURG, VIRGINIA.

shops and factories are generally at work; the indomitable energy of your business men is pushing your trade into new sections of country; the City Government is faithfully and economically administered and our City is securely laying deep and broad the foundations of her wealth and greatness."

The following extracts are from the Reports for the year ending February 1st, 1886.

From the Board of Fire Commissioners:

"We conclude by stating that the Fire Department is in a high

MESSRS. FAULKNER & CRAIGHILL'S DRUG STORE.
(CORNER OF MAIN AND TENTH STREETS.)

state of efficiency, and that our aim is yet higher and higher, until it is *the best*, and to this end we trust we will be, as in the past, strengthened and supported by your hearty coöperation."

From the Chief of the Fire Department:

"The number of fires and alarms for the past year have exceeded by something over double the number for the year previous, there being in all some seventy-six calls. Fires only in two instances have attained any proportions, viz: at the drug store of Messrs. W. A Strother & Son, October 26, and in which nine-tenths of the damage sustained was inflicted by smoke—an element against which we have no means of combatting; the other at Messrs. Ford, Moorman & Co.'s

Among the Largest Buyers and Handlers of Leaf Tobacco are

HOLT, SCHAEFER & CO.,

who do a large Domestic and Foreign Export Business, buying also in other markets of the State and North Carolina, either for direct shipment, or to re-handle such purchases in their Lynchburg factory, the floor space of which is as large, and probably larger than of any factory in the City. Their factory on Lynch Street runs back 190 feet. Adjoining the same in the rear is a large four-story storage house, and connected with this their Jefferson Street factory, where they

Manufacture Tobacco Extract for Export to Europe,

the whole giving one continuous place of business (fronting on Lynch Street, and in the rear, on Jefferson Street), 264 feet in depth.

With six drying rooms, they have ample facilities to handle large quantities of Tobacco at any season of the year, or in the old-fashioned manner by air-drying. The objectionable features of steam-drying are now, however, entirely overcome by employing only rapid circulation of air, which process has secured such universal favor for their tobaccos, as it is a copy of Nature's process, and preserves not only the toughness and texture of the leaf, but likewise its natural gum and flavor.

As their connection with the Tobacco Business extends for a period of about twenty years (partly in other markets, but for the last ten years identified with the Lynchburg market especially), they command, of course, the confidence of the trade, and their continued success is conclusive proof of that fact.

They do an order business for domestic and foreign markets, both for manufacturers and dealers, in bright as well as dark grades, with both of which the Lynchburg market is so well supplied.

factory, January 5th, at which the loss amounted to some $21,000, about half the property being destroyed, the machinery, as also the two lower stories of the building, valued at $19,500, being rescued from the flames. The damage resulting from the remaining calls, seventy-four in number, footed up only about $10,000."

From the Mayor's Message:

"Our School system continues to show splendid results and a uni-

RESIDENCE OF MR. EDMUND SCHAEFER.
(COURT STREET, NEAR SEVENTH.)

form improvement from year to year. The enthusiastic and efficient Superintendent has bent all his energies to the discovery and putting into operation the most improved method of instruction. In this effort he has been ably seconded by a most efficient corps of teachers, both white and colored, and the result is highly gratifying. During the past session there was an enrollment of 2,717 pupils out of a school

population of 6,290. The average daily attendance has been 2,010; the numbers of teachers is 47. * * * I think the City is to be congratulated on having schools equal to any in the country.

* * * * * * *

"In conclusion, the prosperity of your City continues. Many commodious and handsome buildings are in the course of erection; trade is good; the kindly relations hitherto existing between employer and employee have been undisturbed, and your municipal affairs have been faithfully and honestly administered."

BUILDING OF THE "LYNCHBURG VIRGINIAN."
(CORNER OF MAIN AND TENTH STREETS.)

The subjoined are taken from the Reports for the year ending February 1st, 1887—very recently published:

From the Finance Committee:

"It must not be overlooked that from 1881 up to 1885, both inclusive, $1,000,000 was expended in the various departments, principal among which were the permanent improvements on the streets (over $280,000), and water (over $390,000), fire (over $70,000), sewers (over $15,000)."

THE SOUTHERN JEWELRY HOUSE,

F. D. JOHNSON & SON,

802 Main Street, Lynchburg, Virginia.

This well-known house, which has done more than its share towards spreading and establishing the fame of Lynchburg in distant parts of the country as an enterprising commercial centre, was founded by Mr. F. D. Johnson, in 1854, in the town of Culpeper, Virginia. After twenty years of patient, but unremitting labor, Mr. Johnson had acquired that experience which comes sooner or later to all honest and persevering business men, and had become an adept at his trade. He had moreover reduced the mercantile department to a scientific method, which, combined with his unvarying custom of dealing in only such goods as he could safely guarantee, and charging his customers an even and low percentage of profit upon net cost prices, soon had the effect of increasing his business to such a gratifying extent that Culpeper was not large enough to hold it. Accordingly, in 1881, Mr. Johnson moved his establisment to Lynchburg, and in the following year admitted his son, Mr. J. B. Johnson, to partnership. Since that time the operations of the firm—in its wholesale, retail and manufacturing departments—have multiplied with astonishing rapidity, and its order book, representing sales in all the Southern States, as well as in New York, Massachusetts, Connecticut, Rhode Island, and even as far away as Colorado and New Mexico, shows an average of 4,000 orders a year. The firm, moreover, does as good a trade in almost every other State in the South as it does in Virginia. The Repairing Department receives an average of 1,500 crippled watches from outside points during the year, and the house dispatches over 2,000 registered packages per annum through the post-office. These figures give but a faint idea of the volume of business transacted by Messrs. Johnson & Son, which foots up annually to the handsome total of about $65,000. They supply all the principal colleges of the South with medals, badges, &c., and make a specialty of engraving, designing, and such work as monograms and other designs, illustrated catalogues of which will be sent free to any address on application. The other specialties of the firm are Diamonds, Watches, Clocks, Jewelry, Solid Silver and Quadruple-Plated Ware, Spectacles and Eye Glasses, Gold and Silver Headed Canes and Umbrellas. All their Diamond Work, Medals, &c., are designed and manufactured on the premises, and hundreds of testimonials in their possession bear abundant evidence to the universal approval with which their work and their goods have met throughout the vast field covered by their trade. The "F. D. Johnson Watch" is justly celebrated as one of the very best time-keepers manufactured in this country.

From the City Engineer:

"From the record kept at the pump house, it is ascertained that two of the pumps were operated at an average of twenty hours per day, and the steam pump about five hours. The calculated quantity of water pumped the whole year is about 740,000,000 gallons or over 2,000,000 gallons per day. (The pumping capacity is 4,000,000 gallons per day). * * * The pumps, reservoirs and superstructures have been inspected and found to be in a fair and serviceable condition."

MESSRS. F. D. JOHNSON & SON'S JEWELRY STORE.
(802 MAIN STREET.)

From the Chief of the Fire Department:

"We have been called upon only forty-six times, or thirty less than the year previous. In but one instance have the flames assumed any magnitude—this at the factory of Messrs. Wright & Craighill—and which had attained such headway when the alarm was given as to be beyond the power of mortals to suppress. The loss in this instance amounted to some $24,000. In the remaining forty-five cases, only some $5,000 was lost, a total of only about $29,000 for the year; a very moderate sum as compared with the immense losses heralded almost daily from every section of the country."

(ESTABLISHED IN 1865.)

THE FIRST NATIONAL BANK,

OF LYNCHBURG, VIRGINIA.

Capital Stock: $150,000. Surplus and Undivided Profits: $62,000.

JOHN F. SLAUGHTER, *President.* JAMES M. BOOKER, *Vice-President*
ALLEN W. TALLEY, *Cashier.*

DIRECTORS:

CHARLES W. STATHAM, TAYLOR BERRY, J. R. CLARK,
N. R. BOWMAN, JOHN H. LEWIS, J. SINGLETON DIGGS,
JAMES BOYD, JAMES W. WATTS, E. A. CRAIGHILL.

This Bank is one of the oldest monetary institutions in Lynchburg, having been founded immediately after the close of the civil war. It has been uniformly conducted upon conservative business principles, and has never shown the least symptons of weakness or embarrassment, even during the dark days of 1873, when so many banks succumbed to the fury of the financial storm. The First National has made handsome profits for its shareholders, and has also accumulated large security for its depositors. Its stock is therefore very rarely found on the market, although always in strong demand at a high premium. Its dividends have averaged over 10 per cent. per annum during the whole term of its existence. It is to such sound and substantial corporations as the First National Bank that Lynchburg owes, in a large measure, her commercial stability and well established reputation.

FINANCIAL.

The bonded debt of the City, as shown by the Auditor's Report, was on February 1st, 1884, $1,020,132.10; on February 1st, 1885, it was $1,0'9 532.10; on February 1st, 1886, it was $1,106,532.10; and on Februrry 1st, 1887, it was $1,154,092 76. The debt has therefore increased $134,850 within the last four years; but when it is remembered that during that period many vast and valuable improvements have been accomplished—such as the building of the

COLLEGE HILL RESERVOIR.
(BUILT IN 1877.)

magnificent new Reservoirs on Clay Street, at a cost of $100,000; the acquisition of the Gamewell Fire Alarm System and the Electric Light for the streets; the organization of a thoroughly effective paid Fire Department, and a perfect system of Sewerage—it will at once be evident that, in the words of the Finance Committee, in their Report to the City Council, "the means for paying your debt is therefore provided for in your charter, and is self-adjusting." While the public debt has increased, taxation has remained undisturbed, consequent upon the largely enhanced value of property.

EDUCATION.

The City of Lynchburg possesses forty-four Free Schools, of which twenty-six are devoted to the education of white, and eighteen to that of colored children. In addition to these there are seventy-nine Free Schools in Campbell County—forty-nine for white, and thirty for colored children.

There are also a number of excellent private schools for both sexes in and near the City; while the University of Virginia, Washington and Lee University, the Virginia Military Institute, Hampden Sydney College, and other eminent seats of learning are within a radius of sixty miles.

THE LYNCHBURG FAIR.

The Lynchburg Agricultural and Mechanical Society, organized in 1869, has extensive grounds and buildings, in the southwestern suburbs of the City, where Fairs are held annually in the month of October. These Fairs attract large numbers of farmers and others from every quarter of the State, who bring their finest horses, cattle, sheep, hogs, fruit and other farm poducts for exhibition. Large sums are distributed by the Society in the form of premiums, and it is safe to say that in no part of Virginia are the annual fairs better attended, and that nowhere else are finer specimens of live stock and agricultural produce exhibited. All praise is due to the enterprise and public spirit of the gentlemen forming this Association, a fuller account of which will be found in the later pages of this volume

HOTELS AND BOARDING HOUSES.

The City is well provided with excellent Hotels and Boarding Houses, at which the cost of living varies from $50 to $20 a month, according to the accommodation required. Special rates are given to families. By the day the charges range from $1.50 to $3.

WATER POWER.

The James River is a rapid stream, averaging at Lynchburg about six hundred feet in width and four feet in depth. A series of dams, at and above the City, afford a fall of about twenty feet. This magnificent water power, which is available at both sides of the river, is only partially utilized for manufacturing purposes, although the entire volume of the river can easily be made available. This water is owned by the City, and will be furnished as required at a nominal charge.

At many points in the vicinity, both above and below the City, there are splendid sites for mills, furnaces, and factories of various kinds.

COMMERCIAL GROWTH.

The wide extent of rich back country and the excellent facilities for transportation always enjoyed by Lynchburg, gave her, from the beginning, a heavy commission and retail business, under the influence of which she was steadily advancing in population and wealth up to the period of the civil war. Situated in the midst of the finest tobacco-growing region in the world, her people early gave their attention to the manufacture of this article, in which they attained great celebrity, and it was to this special branch of industry that the City chiefly owed her commercial importance.

During the last twenty years of restored peace, Lynchburg has resumed her onward march with renewed energy and with such phenomenal success that she is to-day, in proportion to her population, the wealthiest city, except one, in the United States.

But her prominence is no longer attributable exclusively to the popularity of her brands of manufactured tobacco, nor even to the immense quantity and supurb quality of the leaf handled on her warehouse floors—although in the latter respect she stands at the head of the list of great tobacco markets.

Of late years she has given much attention to and invested much capital in miscellaneous industries, also—such as iron works, furnaces, nail works, fertilizer factories, refrigerators, bark mills, barytes factories and other similar establishments, which give employment to large numbers of men, women and boys, who would otherwise find it difficult to earn a livelihood—to say nothing of the cigarette factories which give honest and lucrative employment to hundreds of white girls.

Nor is this all. The New Lynchburg is the home of enormous business houses which conduct only a wholesale trade, besides others which are wholesale as well as retail dealers. Prior to 1865, commercial travellers—or "drummers"—hailing from the "Tobacco City," were almost unknown quantities, whereas now they are familiar and welcome visitors throughout the South and Southwest, representing such departments of trade as Dry Goods, Drugs and Medicines, Boots and Shoes, Groceries, Fertilizers, and the like. Millions of dollars pour into the City annually through these channels, and the pronounced success with which they have met is sufficient proof that they can compete triumphantly with any of the vaunted Northern and Western markets.

BIGGER'S PUBLIC SCHOOL BUILDING.
(CORNER OF FIFTH AND CLAY STREETS.)

LOCAL INDUSTRIES.

Besides the handling and manufacture of the "seductive weed," and the several other important industries carried on in and around the City, namely: iron works, foundries, flour mills, barytes mills, door and sash factories, sumac mills, fertilizer factories, ice factories and others, already in successful operation, some new enterprises, of which mention will be made hereafter, are about to be undertaken by local capitalists. There is here a wide field for skill and capital, with every reasonable prospect for its remunerative investment in the de-

THE

NORVELL-ARLINGTON HOUSE.

LEADING HOTEL.

Recently Enlarged and Renovated.

CENTRALLY SITUATED ON CHURCH and EIGHTH STREETS.

Near the Post-Office, Court House, Banks, Churches, and other Places of Interest, Usually Sought by Visitors. One Square from Main St. and Street Car Line.

TABLE AND ACCOMMODATIONS FIRST-CLASS.

LARGE SAMPLE ROOMS ON GROUND FLOOR.

Rooms With Baths. Steam Heat and Electric Bells.

OMNIBUS AND BAGGAGE WAGONS AT ALL TRAINS.

R. S. TERRY, Proprietor,

velopment of the numerous sources of industrial wealth not heretofore attempted in this favored locality. An examination of the map will show that, as a point for the collection of raw material and the distribution of manufactured articles, no better place than Lynchburg can be chosen.

GOLDEN OPPORTUNITIES.

With capital sufficient to purchase the requisite plant, and the skill and experience necessary to direct its judicious application—with

THE NORVELL-ARLINGTON HOUSE.
(CORNER CHURCH AND EIGHTH STS.)

cheap and plentiful labor, combined with unsurpassed facilities for transportation—there is no reason why Lynchburg should not attain as high a reputation for her manufactured productions of iron, cotton, wool, paper, glass, wood, cotton-seed oil, boots, shoes, &c., as she has reached in the manufacture of tobacco. A cordial welcome awaits all who may be attracted to this inviting field of enterprise, together with the material aid and support of the municipal authorities and the community at large.

SUMMER RESORTS.

The country immediately to the west of Lynchburg abounds with mineral springs of various kinds, and all possessing special sanitary value. They are sources alike of health, pleasure and profit, and are justly entitled to at least brief mention in Lynchburg's "Sketch Book." Scores of these delightful summer resorts in the Piedmont District, Blue Ridge and Alleghany Mountains are accessible in a few hours by rail from this City. Many of them are exceedingly beautiful and handsomely equipped for the accommodation of from five hundred to a thousand or more visitors. Some of the most attractive of these charming sanatoriums are the Blue Ridge Springs, Yellow Sulphur, White Sulphur, Salt Sulphur, Red Sulphur, Alleghany, Sweet, Rockbridge Alum, Coyners, the Hot, Warm and Healing Springs, &c. These watering places afford good markets for the surrounding country during the summer season, and Lynchburg participates largely in the trade derived from these sources.

To the tourist, this section of Virginia offers many and various attractions. Amongst the most noted curiosities of nature within easy reach of Lynchburg are the Natural Bridge, the Peaks of Otter, the Caverns of Luray, the Natural Tunnel and the Falls of James River, where it breaks through the Blue Ridge Mountains.

GAME AND HUNTING.

The forests, fields and streams of this pleasant region all supply an abundance of game for the sportsman. As a rule, the woods are tolerably free from undergrowth, and are, therefore, easily traversed on foot or on horseback. The squirrel, wild turkey and pheasant are very plentiful in the neighboring forests. Partridges (quail) are very numerous, as also woodcocks. Wild ducks of several varieties are found in large numbers on all the rivers and streams.

Good deer hunting can be had in the Blue Ridge and Alleghany Mountains. Trout abound in most of the mountain streams, and in the large rivers there is excellent bait fishing for chub, perch, pike, &c. Foxes, both red and gray, are found all over Virginia, and furnish capital sport to those fond of "riding to hounds." But they are not in such numbers as to be troublesome or destructive.

CEREALS.

The soil of the "Hill Country" of Virginia, which embraces that region most directly tributary to Lynchburg, varies from light sandy loam to stiff heavy clay. The more closely it approaches the latter the more highly it is esteemed, particularly for mixed farming and grazing. The principal crops raised in this district are tobacco, wheat, corn, oats and hay; but all the grasses, grains, fruits and vegetables common to the temperate zone flourish here with ordinary care. The flour made from wheat grown in this section is considered the best in America, and brings the highest price in the markets where it is known. For many years it was considered the only flour that could be shipped through tropical latitudes without deterioration, and it still maintains its undoubted superiority in the markets of the West Indies and South America. On suitable land, with proper tillage, from twenty to thirty bushels of wheat per acre may reasonably be expected.

In the James River Valley the "bottom" lands will yield, without manuring, from sixty to a hundred bushels of Indian corn per acre. On uplands of good quality, forty to fifty bushels would be considered a good yield. The oat crop usually succeeds corn, requires but slight preparation of the land, grows luxuriantly and yields—especially on bottom or moist lands—a good return to the farmer.

Tobacco requires soil of the best natural quality, or the land must be highly manured, to afford a paying crop; but, when skillfully managed, and under favorable circumstances, it returns a very large profit to the planter. Hay also yields an abundant crop, and finds a ready sale in this and other markets.

FRUIT CULTURE.

The fruits of this division of Virginia are unsurpassed in quality and variety. The apple ripens from June to November, and the later varieties can easily be kept until the succeeding crop can be gathered. This is the home of the famous "Albemarle Pippin" and the beautiful "Lady Apple," so highly and universally esteemed at home and abroad. Besides these, there are many other kinds of apples of excellent quality and prolific fruition. Apples, pears, peaches, plums, cherries, grapes, strawberries, &c., grow freely and require no protection during the winter months.

The grape flourishes with a luxuriance not surpassed by the choicest vineyards in other sections of this country, or those of France and Germany. The eastern slopes of the Blue Ridge Mountains furnish many thousands of acres suited to the cultivation of fruits, including those of the choicest and most delicate varieties, which here attain the highest perfection. Experiments have proved that a better wine can be produced on these mountain slopes than has yet been made elsewhere in the United States.

The Superintendent of "Garden and Grounds," connected with the

UNITED STATES COURT HOUSE AND POST OFFICE.
(ON CHURCH STREET, NEAR NINTH.)

Department of Agriculture, in his Annual Report to Congress for 1869, speaking of "the most healthy grape of the Northern States," says:

"Of course its quality is greatly improved by the length and geniality of the season of growth; for example, those who are familiar with

the fruit only as a production of Massachusetts would not recognize its flavor and vinous character as ripened in Virginia. * * * The mountain slopes and plateaus in Virginia and other Southern States must be looked upon as the great producing regions of this Continent for a certain class of fine wines, not excepting California and other favored sections of the Pacific Coast. We must depend upon this section for the 'coming wine-grape.'"

GRAZING LANDS.

The "Hill Lands" are not excelled by any other part of Virginia, Kentucky or the West as a grazing country. Here are "blue grass"

COURT STREET METHODIST EPISCOPAL CHURCH.
(CORNER OF SEVENTH STREET.)

tracts, watered by plentiful springs and streams of cool soft water, where cattle can feed the whole year round, and where neither hostile Indians nor wild beasts exist to disturb or destroy them.

Mr. J. R. Dodge, of the United States Department of Agriculture, after enumerating the most favored regions in the Eastern and Northern States, the Mississippi Valley and the eastern and western slopes of the Rocky Mountains, makes the following comparison: "But there is one other section, easy of access and superior in the quality of its grasses to any heretofore mentioned, with a climate mild and equable, in which the very finest and best samples of wool in the United States

W. A. STROTHER & SON,

WHOLESALE, RETAIL & MANUFACTURING DRUGGISTS

The senior member of this firm established the business in the year 1855, and has remained continuously in the occupation of the same premises—No. 904 Main Street—ever since that date. "Strother's Drug Store" may therefore be fairly regarded as among the "ancient landmarks" which commemorate the birth, growth and development of Lynchburg's commercial and industrial history. Mr. Strother had already built up a flourishing trade when the civil war broke out, in 1861. In common with his patriotic fellow-countrymen, Mr. Strother volunteered his services to the Confederate cause. For a time his business operations were, to some extent, suspended, but on the restoration of peace, in 1865, they were resumed with renewed energy, and within the last twenty years the volume of his trade has more than quadrupled.

In 1881, Mr. Strother admitted to partnership his son, Mr. W. M. Strother, and the firm assumed its present name. Besides dealing in the commodities common to all first-class wholesale and retail drug houses, the Messrs. Strother are extensive manufacturers of a number of their own recipes, including general family medicines, a full line of flavoring extracts, pills, liniments, horse powders, &c.; while among their more famous specialties, "Silver Medal Cologne" and "Strother's Dentaline" find a ready market in all parts of the Union —over six hundred gross of the former having been sold and shipped to distant points during the past year. Messrs. W. A. Strother & Son are also the patentees of a lubricant which has established itself in the favor of plug tobacco manufacturers throughout the country. It is to such houses as that under review that Lynchburg owes its high mercantile reputation, and the community, being "wise in its generation," extends to it substantial evidence of its confidence and approval. This is the oldest house in the City engaged in the drug business, and the only one that ante-dates the civil war.

have been grown." He then directs attention to this locality, and says it is "the chosen habitat of the blue grass and white clover, whose valleys and slopes and summits are alike fresh with verdure. Scarcely better known to the country at large than the fastnesses of the Rocky Mountains, the lands but little higher in price, this region should produce large quantities of the finest and best merino wool in the United States, and the production of mutton, in view of proximity to markets and abundance and quality of subsistence supplies, could scarcely be undertaken elsewhere with equal advantage."

MR. JOHN W. CARROLL'S RESIDENCE.
(ON HARRISON STREET, CORNER ELEVENTH.)

THE JAMES RIVER VALLEY.

From the discovery of the country to the present day, this beautiful Valley has been universally regarded as the best portion of Virginia. The James River traverses the State from the Alleghany Mountains to the Atlantic Ocean, intersecting the Mountain, Valley, Piedmont and Tide-water Districts, thus embracing within its influence every advantage of climate, soil and production to be found in the State. The scenery along the river, particularly in the hill district, is unsurpassed in variety and beauty. The cool, bracing atmosphere in the

THE "Lone Jack" Cigarette Co.

have moved for the third time into larger quarters, to accommodate their constantly increasing business, and are now located on Clay Street near Twelfth, where they are prepared for a larger business than ever before. They have already, with one exception only, the largest cigarette trade in the State, and if their former ratio of increase continues, will soon take their place among the few large cigarette factories of the United States.

As their name implies, the "Lone Jack" is their leading cigarette. Others are also becoming favorites, the "Ruby" especially. All their brands are free from drugs, or any adulteration, but made of the sweetest bright North Carolina and Virginia tobacco obtainable. Especial mention must be made of an entirely new departure—a long, pure Havana cigarette in brown tobacco paper, the "La Hidalguia" Cigarette, made of Havana tobacco exclusively, of their own importation and selected by Sanderson & Co., Havana, the owners and original manufacturers of this brand. While these cigarettes may be too substantial for the general cigarette smoker, they satisfy another class—the cigar smoker—giving him a better, a genuine Havana, and at the same time a cheaper, smoke than most low-priced cigars. The advertising matter used by the Company has been unique, because combining taste and elegance with usefulness; we refer especially to the elegant brass plaque clocks, known all over the South and West, given free with the Lone Jack Cigarettes.

Among the advantages of this business to the City we wish to mention especially the fact that it gives employment to a large number of girls, who in former years had no field of labor, or at best, a very limited one in this city. The Company employ a number of these, not only for packing and handling the cigarettes, box-making, &c., but for making millions of cigarette holders, with paraffined tips, which have added so much to the popularity of the celebrated Lone Jack Cigarettes.

The principal stockholders are Mr. John W. Carroll, the owner of the world-renowned "Lone Jack" smoking tobacco brand; Edmund Schaefer, of Holt, Schaefer & Co.; the President of theCompany; and R. H. Wright, former partner of W. Duke, Sons & Co., Durham, Manager.

vicinity of the mountains is a complete protection against every form of malarial disease, and is invigorating to the most delicate and sensitive constitutions. It is this portion of the James River Valley that undoubtedly possesses the greatest charms to new settlers of all classes. Here the sturdy farmer in search of a healthy, rich and attractive "plantation;" the lover of nature and field sports; the man of ample means and cultivated taste; the experienced and enterprising manufacturer in

GARLAND'S HILL AND BLACKWATER CREEK.
(FROM NORTHWEST END OF CHURCH STREET.)

pursuit of gain—all may alike find the highest enjoyment and prosperity. Nature has been so lavish in her gifts to this happy valley, and its inhabitants have at all times found it so easy to obtain the comforts and luxuries of life, that its rich stores of timber and minerals have hitherto been comparatively neglected—or at least they have remained practically undeveloped. During the past few years, however, these dormant sources of wealth have attracted considerable

attention, and it is but reasonable to expect that Lynchburg, with its immense natural advantages, will before long become one of the greatest industrial centres of the New South.

VARIOUS.

The population of Lynchburg is now estimated at about 25,000 souls. By including the immediate suburbs this number would be largely increased. In 1880 the census fixed the population at 15,959:

LYNCHBURG'S FIRST TOBACCO FACTORY.
(ON ELM AVENUE NEAR HORSE FORD ROAD.)

while in 1870, when, five years after the close of the war, the City may be said to have entered upon its second lease of existence, it contained, according to the official census, only 6,825 inhabitants.

Not only has the City kept pace with its rapidly growing population as regards the number of its stores, factories and dwellings, but it has also made ambitious strides in the character of its buildings, and in all other matters tending towards public improvements, having regard to ornamentation as well as to mere utility. No city in the

United States of Lynchburg's size can show handsomer churches, factories, hotels, business blocks, private residences and public buildings. In every direction are to be seen evidences of thrift and enterprise. Wherever the eye may turn, it is greeted by magnificent new structures bearing testimony alike to the wealth and the artistic taste of the community. On the main thoroughfares, as well as in those portions of the City and suburbs devoted to private habitations, busy hands are constantly at work filling up vacancies with sightly stores and factories and dwelling houses. Stately churches raise their tapering spires to the sky, while other sacred buildings, less pretensious, perhaps, bear testimony to the competence, liberality and piety of all classes of citizens.

The City of Lynchburg is indeed fair to look upon, presenting, as she does, an air of health, comfort and prosperity which is well sustained by statistical facts. The scenery within and without her boundaries presents a charming and endless variety of hill and valley, field and forest, natural beauty and artistic embellishment, such as are rarely to be met with in any one locality.

With a rich and productive back country, cheap land, abundant labor, a central position in the most favored region of the Southern Land, an equable and healthy climate, unsurpassed water-power and excellent railroad facilities, and removed by only an inconsiderable distance from the very sources whence the great manufacturing interests of the North draw their principal supplies, Lynchburg offers prospects and inducements to the capitalist such as few localities in the United States can justly present, as a careful perusal of this volume to its end—based, as its statements are, upon official facts and figures exclusively—will fully demonstrate.

HISTORICAL.

EARLY DAYS.

LIKE that of every other American City, the History of Lynchburg is inseparable in its early pages from that of the whole Continent. It will not be necessary, therefore, for the purposes of this SKETCH BOOK to inflict upon the intelligent reader the familiar story of the great navigators, Cabot, Columbus, Amadas, and the rest—not to mention the still more remote, and therefore still less authentic, Madoc—nor need we recount the virtues of the aboriginal tribes, to-wit: the Susquehanocks, Pamaunkees and Chickahominies, with their renowned chieftains, Winginia and Granganameo, Powhatan and Opechankanough—distinguished alike for the euphony of their names and the simple amiability of their dispositions; still less desirable would be the vain attempt to clothe the touching narrative of Pocahontas with some new-found element of romance, or to enlarge upon the thrilling adventures and "hair-breadth 'scapes" of the great original Anglo-American John Smith! Suffice it to say that these worthy people—or others like them—certainly lived and flourished, somewhere in Virginia, and at a period not many centuries prior to the birth of Lynchburg's "oldest inhabitant"—that is, if history and tradition be as trustworthy as some people seem to think.

That the Colony was regarded as a most desirable place of residence, even in the remote days of its first organized settlement, may be gathered from the often-quoted expression of the Captain John Smith above referred to—"Heaven and Earth never agreed better to frame a place for Man's habitation."

At that time the whole of the North American Continent, as far as discovered, went under the general name of Virginia, but as the vast extent of the territory began to be appreciated, it was found expedient to divide it into two sections—North Virginia and South Virginia—the former embracing all the country lying to the northward of the entrance to Chesapeake Bay, and the latter extending southerly from the same point as far as the Cape of Florida.

On March 25th, 1584, letters patent were issued by "Bonnie Queen

Bess," granting the whole American Colony to "that great ornament of the British Nation," Sir Walter Raleigh, who immediately formed a sort of joint-stock company for the purpose of fitting out an expedition to settle his new possessions.

After a long and stormy voyage, this expedition landed, as every schoolboy knows, on Roanoke Island, now a part of North Carolina, and at once opened commercial negotiations with the neighboring Indians, with most profitable results.

Referring to this distant period of Virginia's history, Colonel Wm. Byrd, in his *Westover Manuscripts*, quaintly remarks:

"Amongst other Indian Commodities, they brought over Some of of that bewitching Vegetable, Tobacco. And this being the first that ever came to England, Sir Walter thought that he could do no less than make a present of Some of the brightest of it to His Roial Mistress, for her own Smoaking. The Queen graciously accepted of it, but finding her Stomach sicken after two or three Whiffs, it was presently whispered by the earl of Leicester's Faction that Sir Walter had certainly Poisoned Her. But Her Majesty soon recovering her disorder, obliged the Countess of Nottinghan and all her Maids to Smoak a whole Pipe out amongst them."

So this was the microscopic starting point from which such vast results were to follow, as the tide of time rolled on. The agricultural importance of a large area of Virginia, North Carolina and other States, the wealth of their citizens, and the establishment of many a flourishing town and city within their borders—all these things, and more, are traceable to the discovery, two centuries ago, of a nauseating weed! What power is there even in a wreath of smoke, provided only that it issue from royal lips!

But tobacco was not the only valuable product of spontaneous growth found by the pioneer adventurers in this new Paradise, and reported by them to their friends across the main. Indeed, the accounts given of the Colony by those returning from its shores were so uniformly captivating, that it shortly became the "modish frenzy" to emigrate and share the delights thus lavished by prodigal Nature.

Unfortunately, however, the new settlers were, as a rule, both idle and extravagant, and had been tempted hither chiefly by the prospect of absolute exemption from the necessity for labor, and abundant opportunity for the free indulgence of vice.

Reckless waste and persistent improvidence led, as might have been expected, to numerous disappointments and misadventures, as well as to some very rough treatment at the hands of the savage red-skins. As a consequence, the rage for trans-Atlantic emigration cooled down completely, and was not revived till about the year 1606, when the colonization project received fresh impetus by the admission of the Earl of Southampton and other wealthy speculators into the Company. A hundred picked men were then sent out by the new management and landed at Point Comfort, on the waters of the "Chesapik," where

NINTH (BRIDGE) STREET AND AMHERST HEIGHTS.
(FROM COURT HOUSE HILL.)

they built a fort and managed to stand their ground from that time forward, in spite of—possibly helped by—the blunders of their predecessors.

Many and various were the calamities that subsequently befel the infant Colony, but still it continued to grow in strength and wisdom, and to exert its influence and authority over the tribes of untamed Indians, whose active hostility was a perpetual menace to its existence.

The gradual division of the country into separate colonies, which have since become Sovereign States, belongs to general American History, and need not be enlarged upon here.

MAIN STREET, LOOKING NORTHWEST FROM ELEVENTH STREET.

which were to be governed like their English prototypes; lieutenants were to be appointed, whose special duty it should be to keep a wary eye and a heavy hand upon the hostile Indians; sheriffs, sergeants, bailiffs and other officials were to be elected for the purposes of enforcing the law and administering the local government.

One of these Shires—the only one with which we are at present concerned—was named Warrosquyoake (or Warrosquoyacke, or Warrosquijoake), but this barbarous and unpronounceable appellation was abandoned in 1639, on the occasion of the subdivision of Warrosquyoakeshire into the counties of Isle of Wight, Norfolk and Nansemond.

MR. JAMES I. LEE'S RESIDENCE.
(ON CABELL STREET, DANIEL'S HILL.)

In 1652, Surry County, adjoining Isle of Wight, was formed, and, from portions of these two, the County of Brunswick was set apart in 1720. Lunenburg County was formed from Brunswick in 1746, and, seven years later, Bedford County was carved out of Lunenburg.

CAMPBELL COUNTY SET APART.

Campbell County, in which Lynchburg is situated, was formed from Bedford County in 1784, and named in honor of General William Campbell, a distinguished officer of the American Revolution. In form Campbell County is nearly square, each side being about twenty-five miles long. Its area is about 335,000 acres, or 525 square miles. Its surface is undulating and broken, and its soil very productive. It is bounded on the northwest by the James River and Amherst County; on the northeast by Appomattox County; on the southeast by Charlotte County; on the south by the Staunton River and Halifax and Pittsylvania Counties; and on the west by Bedford County.

The James and Staunton Rivers are navigable far above the county limits for boats, thus opening direct water communication with Chesapeake Bay and Albemarle Sound. In 1840 the population of Campbell County was 21,030, of whom 10,213 were white, 10,045 slaves, and 772 free colored.

Besides the City of Lynchburg, there are several important towns and villages within the boundaries of Campbell County; among which are Rustburg, formerly Campbell Court House, the county seat, about twelve miles to the southward of Lynchburg, Brookneal, Leesville and New London.

Mr. Howe, in his "Historical Collections of Virginia," published in 1856, thus mentions our flourishing City:

"Lynchburg, the fifth town in population in Virginia, is situated on a steep declivity on the south bank of James River, in the midst of bold and beautiful scenery, within view of the Blue Ridge and the Peaks of Otter, and 116 miles westerly from Richmond. This town was established in October, 1786, when it was enacted 'that 45 acres of land, the property of John Lynch, and lying contiguous to Lynch's Ferry, are hereby vested in John Clarke, Adam Clement, Charles Lynch, John Callaway, Achilles Douglass, William Martin, Jesse Burton, Joseph Stratton, Micajah Moorman and Charles Brooks, gentlemen, trustees, to be by them, or any six of them, laid off in lots of half an acre each, with convenient streets, and established a town by the name of Lynchburg.' The father of the above named John Lynch was an Irish emigrant, and took up land here previous to the Revolution. His place, then called Chestnut Hill, afterwards the seat of Judge Edmund Winston, was two miles below here. At his death, the present site of Lynchburg fell to his son John, by whose exertions the town was established. The original founder of Lynchburg was a member of the demonination of Friends, and a plain man, of strict integrity and great benevolence of character. He died about twenty years since, at a very advanced age. At the time of the formation of the Town, there was but a single house, the ferry house, which stood where the toll-house to the bridge now is. A tobacco warehouse and two or three stores were thereupon built under the hill, and it was sometime before any buildings were erected upon the main street. The growth of the place has been gradual. In 1804, a Methodist Episcopal Church was erected upon the site of the present one, and shortly after a market was established. The first Sabbath School in the State was formed in the church above mentioned, in the spring of 1817, by George Walker, James McGehee and John Thurman. The next churches built were the First Presbyterian, the Baptist, the Protestant Episcopal, the Protestant Methodist, the Second Presbyterian and a Friends' meeting house in the outskirts of the town. The Catholic and Universalist Churches were erected in 1843."

FORTY-FIVE YEARS AGO.

In 1843 the *Lynchburg Republican* published the annexed communi-

THE OLD MARKET HOUSE ON NINTH STREET.
(BUILT 1813. REMOVED 1873.)

cation, which is reproduced here for the sake of the interesting statistical information it contains:

"The census of 1840 showed a population of upwards of five thousand. Since that time there has been a considerable accession to the number of buildings, from which we may safely assume that our present population reaches, if it does not exceed, 6,000. The extent of the Tobacco Trade of Lynchburg may be judged of from the fact that upwards of fifteen thousand hogsheads have already been inspected here the present year—a number which far exceeds all previous calculation. We have about thirty tobacco factories and stemmeries,

giving employment to about 1,000 hands; three flouring mills, manufacturing, I am told, about 20,000 barrels of flour annually; one cotton factory, operating 1,400 spindles; iron foundries, which consume, probably, 100 tons pig iron annually. More than 100,-000 bushels of wheat are sold here yearly, 300 tons bar iron, 200 tons pig metal sold to the country; 1,000 tons plaster of Paris. About 50 dry goods and grocery stores—selling in the aggregate, more than one million dollars' worth of goods Some of

COURT STREET, LOOKING NORTHWEST FROM COURT HOUSE.

our stores are so extensive and elegant as not to suffer by a comparison with those of Philadelphia and New York—4 apothecaries and druggists; several cabinet manufactories; 4 saddle and harness manufactories; 10 blacksmith shops; several excellent hotels; 5 jewelers' establishments; 2 printing offices.

"There are here branches of the Bank of Virginia and the Farmers' Bank of Virginia, and also three Savings Banks. Seven flourishing Sabbath Schools, with from 700 to 1,000 scholars. One debating society, with a library of several thousand volumes, &c., &c., &c.

From the hasty view I have presented, and which by no means does justice to the industry and enterprise of our citizens, it will be seen that we have already the elements of a flourishing City. But I have said nothing of the magnificent line of canal, now in the 'full tide of successful experiment,' between this place and Richmond, from which we are distant 147 miles by water. This splendid work, the pride and boast of Virginia, opens to Lynchburg the brightest era which has ever yet dawned upon her fortunes, securing to us a safe, speedy and cheap navigation for the immense produce shipped annually to Richmond and the North—and destined, as the writer believes, to furnish

WATER WORKS DAM AND "LOVER'S LEAP."

a great thoroughfare for the countless thousands of produce and merchandise for the western and southwestern part of our State, as well as Tennessee, Alabama, &c."

"LYNCH LAW."

With regard to the origin of this judicial eccentricity, or rather of the name by which it is now universally recognized, several theories have been advanced. Local tradition has ascribed it to the justifiable, if lawless, methods of enforcing the social virtues, practiced by a member of the Lynch family of this neighborhood, one of whom founded the City; and this opinion seems to have been unhesitatingly adopted by Mr. Howe, who thus expresses it in his *Historical Collections:*

"Col. Charles Lynch, a brother of the founder of Lynchburg, was an officer of the American Revolution. His residence was on the Staunton, in the southwest part of this County, now the seat of his grandson, Charles Henry Lynch, Esq. At that time this country was very thinly settled, and infested by a lawless band of tories and desperadoes. The necessity of the case involved desperate measures, and Col. Lynch, then a leading Whig, apprehended and had them punished, without any superfluous legal ceremony. Hence the origin of the term *Lynch Law*. This practice of *lynching* continued years after the war, and was applied to many cases of mere suspicion of guilt, which could not be regularly proven. 'In 1792,' says Wirt's Life of Henry, 'there were many suits on the south side of James River for inflicting Lynch's law.' At the battle of Guildford Court House, a regiment of riflemen, raised in this part of the State, under the command of Col. Lynch, behaved with much gallantry. The Colonel died soon after the close of the war. Charles Lynch, a Governor of Louisiana, was his son."

But alas for the infallibility of local tradition and the unanimity of local opinion! Referring to the above, a correspondent of the Lynchburg *Virginian* writes to that paper, on November 20th, 1886, over the initial "W," as follows:

* * * * *

"This Colonel Charles Lynch was a brother to John Lynch, after whom our city was named. They were the sons of John Lynch, who came from Ireland and took up lands in this vicinity. He is said to have come from Limerick.

"Now the reading of this article recalled to my mind a different and more remote origin of the term 'Lynch Law,' which I remember to have seen many years ago.

"The story was to this effect: Many years ago, the Mayor of Limerick, named Lynch, was a merchant of high character, stern integrity, and an abiding sense of justice, a man of great popularity and of unblemished credit.

"He was accustomed to buy largely from Spanish merchants, and upon one occasion sent his own son to Spain to lay in a cargo of goods; but the young man, finding the fascinations and pleasures around him too strong for his self-control, wasted the money entrusted to him, and was forced, in shame, to go to the merchants with whom he had left orders, and countermand them, saying he could not make payment. Their reply was: 'The credit of your house is too good and well-established for us to refuse to send the goods, and we will ship them and send our agents along with you, and your house can make payment to them upon their arrival, or at such time as it may prefer.' To this the young man agreed, and so they set out upon their voyage. But, in mid-ocean, he concluded to throw the agents overboard, and so escape payment and the indignation of his father. But, upon his arrival in port, his father heard the story from some of the crew, and immediately had his son arrested and confined in his own castle, a stronghold.

"The citizens, upon hearing this fact, assembled around the castle and demanded the release of the son. The stern but just old father said to them that, in his official capacity, he knew no man's son, and that

RESIDENCES ON COURT STREET.
DR. E. A. CRAIGHILL. MR. R. T. CRAIGHILL.

it should not be said of him that he, who always endeavored to support the majesty of the law, would be less exacting in his measure of justice because it was his own son who was the offender. He was told in return that his son should not be brought to trial for the murder of the Spaniards, and that, unless he opened the castle doors they would be broken down. The father, thus seeing that the law would be wrenched out of his hands, placed a halter round the neck of his son and had him suspended from the window above the heads of the infuriated citizens. This summary execution, without the form of trial, was then and there called 'Lynch Law.'

R. R. GOODMAN,

—— MANUFACTURER OF ——

Tobacco Hogsheads, Tierces, Cases

AND ALL KINDS OF PACKING BOXES.

HOGSHEAD

STAVES.

LINING.

HOOPS AND

PLANING MILL AND WOOD WORKING MACHINERY.

Flooring, Ceiling and Lumber Dressed at Short Notice.

BRACKETS. WINDOW AND DOOR FRAMES. SCROLL SAWING.

MOULDINGS. STORE FRONTS, &c.

MILL, YARDS AND OFFICE:

1300 to 1310 JEFFERSON STREET,

LYNCHBURG, VA.

"Your correspondent chanced to mention the above account to a gentleman of much intelligence, born in Ireland, who replied that he was familiar with the story, having heard it many years ago.

"It now occurs to me, that as the above-named Charles Lynch, of Revolutionary memory, the originator of this form of justice here, was of Irish parentage, he had learned this story of his own namesake—and, maybe, progenitor—of Limerick, and so determined to introduce into America this Irish form of justice."

THE BIRTH PLACE OF THE CELEBRATED "LONE JACK."
(IN REAR OF NEW FACTORY—TWELFTH STREET.)

And alas, again, for the stability of the claim thus set up for Limerick, as having given to the world a new code of judicial procedure and to the dictionary a new word! As regards the latter, however, it cannot be denied that the Emerald Isle is quite equal to the achievement, as witness the frequent and general adaptation of the modern "boycott."

On the subject under discussion, the *Encyclopedia Britanica*, (vol. xv, p. 105) pronounces as follows—and in so doing furnishes evidence of careful research and impartial judgment:

"Lynch Law, a term used in the United States to characterize the action of private individuals, organized bodies of men, or disorderly mobs, who, without legal authority, proceed to punish, by hanging or otherwise, real or suspected criminals, without a trial according to the ordinary forms of law. The origin of the term is doubtful. American lexicographers generally refer it to the practice of a Virginia farmer of the 17th century, named Lynch, who, when he caught a wrong-doer, was wont to tie him to a tree and flog him, without waiting to summon the officers of the law. He is also said to have acted, by

CITY HALL AND COURT HOUSE.

request of his neighbors, though without any legal authority, as a judge in the summary trial of persons accused of crime. Others trace the origin of the name to the act of James Fitzstephen Lynch, mayor and warden of Galway, Ireland, in 1493, who is said to have 'hanged his own son out of the window for defrauding and killing strangers, without martial or common law, to show a good example to posterity.' Others trace it still further to the old Anglo-Saxon verb *linch*, meaning to beat with a club, to chastise, &c., which they assert has survived in this cognate meaning in America, as have many other words and expressions long obsolete in Great Britain."

But, however thickly veiled in mystery the true origin of "Lynch Law" may be, or may be destined to remain, and whether it was really indigenous to this fair region of the Old Dominion or not, it must be comforting to the patriotic Lynchburger to feel that the fame of his City need not rely entirely upon the final unravelling of this knotty

question. There can at least be no doubt as to the fact that Lynchburg has given birth to other equally famous and much more creditable progeny, about whose paternity there is no room for argument. Among these may be mentioned "Lone Jack," whose excellence is familiar to every consumer of the "Celestial weed" in every quarter of the globe—alike within the frozen belt of the Polar Zone and beneath the scorching rays of the tropical sun—in the mining camp of the Far West and on the sheep run of the Antipodes. There are other articles of commerce, also distinctively the offspring of Lynch-

ST. PAUL'S (PROTESTANT EPISCOPAL) CHURCH.
(CHURCH STREET, CORNER OF SEVENTH.)

burg, which have rendered her name sweetly familiar in every State and Territory of the Union, such as "Silver Medal Cologne," the fragrant product of one Main Street Drug Establishment, and "Camm's Emulsion," manufactured at another; there is "Phertiston," the magical fertilizer and insecticide; and there are many more names which might be placed upon the roll of honor. But wherefore? This is not the record of a mushroom—born in the night, matured by the morning dew and doomed to perish before noon-day—but of a giant oak, still in its lusty youth—having only attained, as yet, the years of a single century, but already firmly rooted as the hills upon which it stands.

E. E. ROSS,

GENERAL CONTRACTOR AND BUILDER,

MANUFACTURER OF

All Kinds of Builders' Material.

SASH. BLINDS. DOORS. MOULDINGS.

Scroll Work of all Descriptions.

DOOR AND WINDOW FRAMES, &c.

Stairways IN EVERY VARIETY.

NEWEL POSTS, AND Balusters

SLAVERY AND TOBACCO.

The following extract, relating to the inception and growth of the slave trade and the early cultivation of tobacco, with their influence on the character, manners and general condition of the inhabitants of Colonial Virginia, will afford interesting and instructive reading to those who are not already familiar with the subject. It is drawn from the "Life of Jefferson," by Prof. George Tucker, of the University of Virginia,—a work of high merit, having been written with great perspicuity and ingenuous fidelity, elucidating, as it does, incidentally, many important points in the civil, political and commercial history of the State.

"In 1744, at the period of the birth of Mr. Jefferson, the settlement had extended about 200 miles from the sea-coast, and, in the northern part of the Colony, had passed the Blue Ridge. The population was then about 200,000, of whom from a quarter to a third were slaves.

"The cultivation of tobacco and the introduction of slaves, soon after Virginia was settled, have had a marked influence upon the habits, character and fortunes of the country. The introduction of tobacco in England, about twenty years before the settlement of Jamestown, led to a rapid extension of its use. A demand being thus created, and a heavy price paid, encouraged the first settlers of Virginia to cultivate it for market, to the neglect of other crops. It long continued the sole article of export, and, from the inadequate supply of the precious metals, it became the general measure of value, the principal currency of the Colony. In 1758, the quantity exported had increased to about seventy millions of pounds, since which time the product has somewhat diminished.

"As this plant requires land of the greatest fertility, and its finer sorts are produced only in virgin soil, which it soon exhausts, its culture has been steadily advancing westwardly, where fresh land is more abundant, leaving the eastern region it has impoverished to the production of Indian corn, wheat and other grain. Its cultivation has thus generally ceased in the country below the falls of the great rivers, and, in its progress to the west, the centre of the tobacco region is now two hundred miles from the coast.

"The business of cultivating tobacco and preparing it for market requires such continual attention, and so much and so many sorts of handling, as to allow to the planter little time for any of the other useful processes of husbandry; and thus the management of his dairy and orchard, and the useful operations of manuring, irrigation and cultivating artificial grasses, are either conducted in a slovenly way or neglected altogether. The tobacco district nowhere exhibits the same external face of verdure, or marks of rural comfort and taste, as are to

—THE—

Virginia Nail and Iron Works Company.

E. SCHAEFER, President. T. C. JONES, General Manager.
CHAS. M. BLACKFORD, Vice President. J. P. WILLIAMS, Sec'y. and Treas.

Though the works are not in the City itself, this is nevertheless a Lynchburg enterprise, and, outside its tobacco factories, the most important manufacturing establishment connected with the City and its trade.

The works are located about four miles above the City; the "big dam" which spans the wide James just above their works, gives them the water power of the whole river, sufficient for several works as large as theirs, but as the Company own the whole tract of land along the river from the dam to the next lock, these advantages will remain secured to them forever. With excellent railroad facilities at their door, located in the midst of the ore lands of the James River Valley, within easy reach of the New River, Clinch Valley and Craig's Creek ore and coal fields, and with this immense water power secured to them forever, the advantage and value of their property cannot be overestimated. In order to fully develop the value of their property, the Company have now determined to add a blast furnace to their works, which will be completed by the end of the year. Making their own iron, they expect to double their profits, at the same time to enlarge the capacity of their works and to extend their trade into new territory. The new stock offered for carrying out these projects was taken up in three days; this fact is proof enough that the Company's advantages and brilliant prospects are fully recognized. The capital stock of the Company is now about $200,000. After their present plans are carried out and the prospective profits realized, further additions to the works are contemplated.

Their present capacity is something over 400 kegs of nails per day, besides several tons of bar-iron, spikes, &c. The demand for the products of the mill is greater than it can supply, though working to its full capacity; their nails and iron being of superior quality, are selling not only in Virginia and neighboring States, but as far south as Georgia and Alabama and in Birmingham, even in competition with its own products—in fact in many Southern cities.

By increasing the capacity of their works and cheapening the cost of their product, the Company expect in another year to reach the Mississippi and the Gulf States with their goods.

Altogether their prospects are most promising and we know that the liberal and energetic management of the works will see to it that they are realized as far as in their power.

be seen in those countries in which its culture has been abandoned.

"But the most serious consequence of the tobacco cultivation is to be found in the increase of slaves; for, though it did not occasion their first introduction, it greatly encouraged their importation afterwards. It is to the spirit of commerce, which, in its undistinguished pursuit of gain, ministers to our vices no less than to our necessary wants, that Virginia owes this portentous accession to her population. A Dutch ship from the coast of Guinea, entered James River in 1620, thirteen years after the first settlement of Jamestown, and sold twenty of her slaves to the Colonists.

"The large profits which could be made from the labor of slaves, while tobacco sold at three shillings sterling a pound, equal to about ten times its ordinary price now, greatly encouraged their further importation, by giving to the planters the means of purchasing, as well as

PROPERTY OF THE VIRGINIA NAIL AND IRON WORKS COMPANY.

the inclination; and the effect would have been much greater if they had not been continually supplied with labor from the paupers, and sometimes the convicts, who were brought from England and sold to the planters for a term of years to defray the expenses of their transportation.

"This supply of English servants, together with the gradual fall in the price of tobacco, had so checked the importation of slaves that, in the year 1671, according to an official communication from the Governor, Sir William Berkeley, while the whole population was but 40,000 the number of indented servants was 6,000, and that of the slaves was but 2,000. The importation of the latter, he says, did not exceed two or three cargoes in seven years, but that of servants, of whom, he says, 'most were English, few Scotch and fewer Irish,' he estimates at 1,500 annually.

JACOB H. FRANKLIN. CHAS. M. FRANKLIN. EDGAR FRANKLIN.

JACOB H. FRANKLIN & SONS,

WHOLESALE

Grocers and Commission Merchants,

708 MAIN STREET,

Lynchburg, - - Virginia.

Keep always in store one of the largest and most varied stocks of

Heavy, Staple and Fancy Groceries,

to be found in the State, consisting in part of Coffees, Teas, Sugars, Syrups, Molasses, Bacon, Bulk Meats, Lard, Rice, Hominy, Cheese, Fish, Soaps, Candles, Soda, Bread Powders, Oils, Canned Fruits Vegetables Fish and Meats; Brooms, Buckets, Blacking, Blueing; Cakes, Crackers, Candies; Spices, ground and whole; Concentrated Lye, Potash, Matches, Paper, Paper Bags, Twines, Alum, Copperas, Epsom Salts, Sulphur, &c., &c.

Which they will sell strictly wholesale, as cheap as they can be bought in this or any other market.

THE

Lynchburg Ice and Refrigerator Co.,

E. SCHAEFER, President. JOHN W. CARROLL, Vice President.
P. J. OTEY, Treasurer.

Is a recent addition to the manufacturing establishments of the City. This Company, as the name indicates, make artificial ice, using distilled water, viz., condensed steam, therefore an ABSOLUTELY PURE article is obtained, free from any vegetable or animal germs, which even the best transparent natural ice so often contains. Their capacity is 20,000 pounds per day, more than this in cool weather, something less during the hot weather, when they have to keep the temperature of their ice and cold storage houses down to the freezing point.

Ice in Lynchburg is now selling at ½ cent per pound, in larger quantities at $5 per ton, while in former years the price was about twice as high. The advantage this establishment has been to the City is therefore apparent at a glance. What in most other inland cities of the South is still more or less a luxury, is here selling so low as to bring this—a necessity, almost, in a hot climate—within the reach of all.

"But in process of time slave labor was found preferable to that of indented white servants, partly because the negro slaves were more cheaply fed and clothed than the laborers who were of the same race as the masters, but principally because they were less able to escape from bondage, and were more easily retaken. The colonial statute book affords abundant evidence of the frequency and facility with which the indented servants ran away from their masters; and the extent of the mischief may be inferred from the severity of its punishment. In 1642, runaway servants were liable, for a second offence, to be branded on the cheek; though fifteen years afterwards the law was so far mitigated as to transfer this mark of ignominy to the shoulder. In 1662, their term of service, which did not often exceed four or five years,

RESIDENCE OF MR. P. A. KRISE.
(COR. CHURCH AND SIXTH STREETS.)

might, for the offence of running away, be prolonged, at the discretion of a magistrate, and the master might superadd 'moderate corporeal punishment.' In the following year, this class of persons, prompted by the convicts who had been sent over after the restoration of Charles the Second, formed a conspiracy of insurrection and murder, which was discovered just in time to be defeated. Seven years afterwards, in 1670, the Governor and Council took upon themselves to prohibit the further importation of convicts, whom they call 'jail birds,' and they assign this conspiracy as one of their motives for the order. The privilege, too, enjoyed by the servant, of complaining to the magistrate for the harsh treatment of his master, either as to food, clothing or

WINFREE, ADAMS & LOYD,

MANUFACTURERS OF AND WHOLESALE DEALERS IN

Plug, Twist, and Smoking Tobacco.

THE business enterprise, prosperity and solidity of a City are in a large measure indicated by the extent and character of her commercial houses. In the commerce of the South, the City of Lynchburg occupies a prominent and important position. Her situation, as the natural depot for the reception, manufacture and shipment of tobacco, gives her special prominence in connection with this great staple, which may be considered the main source of the prosperity, wealth and commercial standing of the City.

The old, wealthy and successful establishments engaged in handling and manufacturing tobacco have become familiar by trade and reputation in all sections of the land.

One of these is the firm now under review. In 1867, Mr. C. V. Winfree and Mr. William H. Loyd associated themselves together under the firm name of Winfree & Loyd. The house soon took rank as one of the leading tobacco manufactories in this part of the country—a position to which it was justly entitled from the variety and magnitude of its stock, its extensive transactions, and the well-known characteristics of the gentlemen composing the firm.

About four years ago Mr. Charles L. Adams, who had previously served the firm with faithfulness and ability for many years, was admitted as a partner, and the present name of the firm (Winfree, Adams & Loyd) was adopted.

All the members are practical men, having acquired by long training and experience a thorough knowledge of their work and their business is managed carefully, scientifically, and with the consummate judgment which disdains the use of inferior materials or the offering of anything short of excellence in manufactured articles. The financial part of the concern is managed by the senior partner, while Mr. Loyd attends to buying the raw material at the warehouse sales, and, being a fine judge of qualities, selects the leaf with the utmost care. The filling of orders and active office business is under the immediate supervision of Mr. Adams.

The factory of the firm is situated at the corner of Tenth and Lynch Streets, and comprises two large four-story brick buildings, forming together one commodious and complete establishment, thoroughly equipped with the machinery and appliances necessary for their extensive operations.

The manufacturing business is organized into different departments, managed by competent men, all under the constant direction of the proprietors. Mr. George W. Stanley, who has charge of the manufacturing department, is considered one of the best factory managers and manufacturers in Virginia.

Their trade in manufactured tobacco is extensive throughout all the Southern States, New Orleans especially being one of the principal centres from which their brands are widely distributed. The house deals exclusively and entirely in medium and fine grades of the weed, and the brands they manufacture have become justly popular with consumers.

Their most celebrated brands are "Arkansas Traveller," a 9-inch rich Mahogany plug; "Nectar Leaf," an 11 and 12-inch plug for general use; "Mississippi Sawyer," a great favorite in certain markets; "Cloth of Gold," fine 12-inch plug; "Yum Yum," "Tom and Jerry," "Nip and Tuck," "Jack and Gill," and "Yazoo Belle." The "Eclipse" twist is made from Burley filler and affords an excellent chew. "Fanny Leslie" and "Little Helen" are fine grades of tobacco, also put up in twist form.

In granulated smoking tobacco the firm puts up "Virginia Bride," "Old Virginia," "Southern Puff," and other brands in pounds quarters, eighths and other quantities, as demanded.

The trade of the house is entirely wholesale, and the firm having the best facilities for the prompt fulfillment of orders, is in a position to offer inducements to the trade second to none of its contemporaries, while liberality and fair dealing will be found to characterize all its transactions.

punishment, formed, no doubt, a further ground of preference for slaves, who had no such inconvenient rights.

"Under the united influence of these circumstances, the number of negro slaves so increased that, in 1732, the Legislature thought proper to discourage their further importation, by a tax on each slave imported; and, not to alarm the commercial jealousy of England, the law, conforming to the notions of the age, formally provided for what no mode of levying the tax could have prevented, that the duty should be paid by the purchaser. This duty was at first five per cent. on the value of the slave, but in a few years afterwards, (1740) it was increased to ten per cent. from which it was never reduced. It did not, however, prevent large importations, for we find the number to have increased in 119 years in the ratio of 1 to 146; that is, from 2,000 in the year 1671, to 293,427 in 1790; while in the same period the whites had increased only as 1 to 12, or from 38,000 to 454,881. In the forty years which have elapsed, from the first to the last census, it is gratifying to perceive that the increase of the free population in Virginia has been somewhat greater than that of the slaves, in the proportion of 63 per cent. to 60, and that this comparative gain seems to be gradually increasing.

"As Eastern Virginia is everywhere intersected by navigable rivers, which are skirted on either side by rich alluvial lands, the early settlers, whose plantations were principally along the margins of the rivers, were able to carry on a direct intercourse with foreign countries, from their separate dwellings. Thus commerce, by the very diffusion of its most important natural facilities, did not here concentrate in a few favorable spots and foster the growth of towns, as in most of the other Colonies; and, at the beginning of the Revolution, Williamsburg, the seat of Government, and the largest town in Virginia, itself the most populous of the Colonies, did not contain 2,000 inhabitants. But as the bees which form no hive collect no honey, the commerce, which was thus dispersed, accumulated no wealth. The disadvantages of this dispersion were eventually perceived by the Colonists, and many efforts were made by the Legislature to remedy the mischief by authorizing the establishment of towns on selected sites, and giving special privileges and immunities to those who built or those who resided on them. Their purpose was also favored, and even stimulated, by the Government, from fiscal considerations. But most of these legislative efforts failed, and none were very successful. Thus, in 1680, as many as twenty towns were authorized by Act of Assembly, being one for each County; yet at not more than three or four of the designated spots is there even a village remaining to attest the propriety of the selection.

"There were, indeed, wanting in the Colony all the ordinary constituents of a large town. Here were no manufactories to bring together and employ the ingenious and industrious. The Colonists,

devoting themselves exclusively to agriculture, owned no shipping which might have induced them to congregate for the sake of carrying on their foreign commerce to more advantage; here was no Court, which, by its splendor and amusements, might attract the gay, the voluptuous and the rich; there was not even a class of opulent landlords, to whom it is as easy to live on their rents in town as in the country, and far more agreeable. But the very richest planters all cultivated their own lands with their own slaves; and, while those lands furnished most of the materials of a generous and even profuse hospitality, they could be consumed only where they were produced, and could neither be transported to a distance nor converted into money. The tobacco, which constituted the only article of export, served to pay for the foreign luxuries which the planter required; yet, with his social habits, it was barely sufficient for that purpose, and not a few of the largest estates were deeply in debt to the Scotch or English merchants who carried on the whole commerce of the country. Nor was this system of credit more eagerly sought by the improvident planter than it was given by the thrifty and sagacious trader, for it afforded to him a sure pledge for the consignment of the debtor's crop, on the sales of which his fair perquisites amounted to a liberal profit; and if he was disposed to abuse his trust, his gains were enormous. The merchants were therefore ready to ship goods and accept bills of exchange on the credit of future crops, while their factors in the Colony took care, in season, to make the debt safe by a mortgage on the lands and slaves of the planter. Some idea of the pecuniary thraldom to which the Virginia planter was formerly subjected may be formed from the fact that twice a year, at a general meeting of the merchants and factors in Williamsburg, they settled the price of tobacco, the advance on the sterling cost of goods, and the rate of exchange with England. It can scarcely be doubted that the regulations were framed as much to the advantage of the merchants as they believed it practicable to execute. Yet it affords evidence of the sagacious moderation with which this delicate duty was exercised, that it was not so abused as to destroy itself.

"This state of things exerted a decided influence on the manners and character of the Colonists, untrained to habits of business and possessed of the means of hospitality. They were open-handed and open-hearted; fond of society, indulging in all its pleasures and practicing all its courtesies. But these social virtues also occasionally ran into the kindred vices of love of show, haughtiness, sensuality—and many of the wealthier class were to be seen seeking relief from the vacuity of idleness, not merely in the allowable pleasures of the chase and the turf, but in the debasing ones of cock-fighting, gaming and drinking. Literature was neglected, or cultivated by the small number who had been educated in England, rather as an accomplish-

These gentlemen commenced business in July, 1878, and are the **Pioneers in the Exclusively Wholesale BOOT and SHOE Trade in Lynchburg.** Their business has increased regularly with each season, necessitating a move from one Warehouse to another, to obtain more commodious quarters, until February of 1883, when they moved into the spacious building which they now occupy, **No. 808 Main Street,** (see engraving on page 101), the dimensions of which are 25 feet front by 132 feet deep, five stories high, with all of the modern improvements for the conduct and dispatch of business. They have found it profitable to employ six traveling salesmen, and their house is represented all through the Southern States generally. Their motto from the commencement of their business has been "quick sales and small profits," and to-day they claim to be the leading JOBBING BOOT AND SHOE HOUSE of the OLD DOMINION. Their KIP HAND-MADE WESTERN-IMPROVED BOOT AND SHOE, sold under their guarantee, enjoy a reputation for general utility and durability unequalled by any similar styles of goods on the market.

Among the advantages which this House has are the quick delivery of goods to their customers, being nearer to the trade for which they cater, and the saving of freight to their patrons, which in many instances is less by 2½ to 3 per cent. on an entire bill, than from Northern markets. Recognizing and even realizing the oft-questioned, but nevertheless indisputable and irrefutable argument, that SOUTHERN JOBBING HOUSES, as compared with those in the North and East, hold, in a steadily increasing degree, the vantage ground, based on the fundamental principles of reason and economy, to furnish and supply the SOUTH with her merchandise, **WITT & WATKINS** press forward from season to season with renewed energy and strengthened determination to force their advantages of situation into notice, and their success, as the result of their efforts, continues to grow to a very gratifying extent, as the years come and go.

ment and a mark of distinction than for the substantial benefit it confers.

"Let us not, however, overrate the extent of these consequences of slavery. If the habitual exercise of authority, united to a want of steady occupation, deteriorated the character of some, it seemed to

VIEW ON MAIN STREET. (LOOKING SOUTHEAST FROM SEVENTH STREET.)

give a greater elevation of virtue to others Domestic slavery, in fact, places the master in a state of moral discipline, and, according to the use he makes of it, is he made better or worse. If he exercises his unrestricted power over the slave, in giving ready indulgence to his

ROBERT D. YANCEY,

ATTORNEY-AT-LAW,

LYNCHBURG, - - - VIRGINIA.

TIMBERLAKE, JACKSON & Co.,

MANUFACTURERS OF TOBACCO,

LYNCHBURG, VIRGINIA.

☞ CHEW { *MIGHTY DOLLAR, PALACE CAR,* } *PLUG.* *COON, PONY,* } *NAVY.*

F. A. LEE,

SURGEON DENTIST,

908 *MAIN ST., LYNCHBURG, VA.*

W. M. SEAY,

CONTRACTOR AND BUILDER,

814 *Church Street, Lynchburg, Va.*

CALL FOR ESTIMATES. SATISFACTION GUARANTEED.

W. O. JOHNSON,

DEALER IN

STAPLE and FANCY GROCERIES, CONFECTIONERIES, TOBACCO, CIGARS, &c.

314 Main Street, Lynchburg, Virginia.

Dunsmore's Business College, Staunton, Virginia.

This Institution has been incorporated by the Legislature of the State of Virginia and endorsed by some of her best citizens. It not only teaches young and middle-aged men the theory of Business and Accounting, but each and every one is required to do actual business transactions, as they would have to do in every-day life. They are thoroughly trained in everything pertaining to business life.

STAUNTON, VA., July 30, 1884.

We take pleasure in recommending to the public "Dunsmore's Business College," of this city. We have attended and taken part in several examinations of Mr. Dunsmore's pupils, and can testify to his thoroughness as a teacher, and to the uniform proficiency of his scholars. His pupils are now filling a number of important positions, and his college is destined to take rank among the leading Business Colleges of the country.

THO. A. BLEDSOE, *Cashier Nat. Val. Bank.*
W. P. TAMS, *Cashier Augusta Nat. Bank.*

STAUNTON, VA., May 20, 1886.

* * * You are doing an admirable work and doing it admirably. I do not hesitate to commend you and your institution very heartily.

HERBERT H. HAWES,
Pastor Second Presbyterian Church.

STAUNTON, VA., May 26, 1886.

It gives me pleasure to bear witness to the surpassing merits of Prof. Dunsmore's Business College. He is a born teacher, and his College has no superior.

JAMES NELSON, D. D., *Pastor First Baptist Church.*

humors or caprice—if he habitually yields to impulses of anger, and punishes whenever he is disobeyed, or obeyed imperfectly—he is certainly the worse for the institution which has thus afforded aliment to his evil propensities. But if, on the other hand, he has been taught to curb these sallies of passion or freaks of caprice, or has subjected himself to a course of salutary restraint, he is continually strengthening himself in the virtues of self-denial, forbearance and moderation, and he is all the better for the institution which has afforded so much occasion for the practice of these virtues. (The character of the Presidents which Virginia has furnished may be appealed to for a confirmation of this view; and many living illustrations will readily present themselves to all who have a personal knowledge

FIRST PRESBYTERIAN CHURCH.
(ON MAIN STREET, BETWEEN TWELFTH AND THIRTEENTH.)

of the Southern States.) If, therefore, in a slave-holding country, we see some of the masters made irascible, cruel and tyrannical, we see many others as remarkable for their mildness, moderation and self-command; because, in truth, both the virtues of the one and the vices of the other are carried to the greater extreme by the self-same process of habitual exercise."

MUNICIPAL.

In the year 1880, the City Ordinances of Lynchburg were revised and arranged by the then City Attorney, Capt. Charles M. Blackford,

G. A. COLEMAN & CO.,

—DEALERS IN—

BOOTS, SHOES, HATS, TRUNKS, &c., &c.

714 MAIN STREET, LYNCHBURG, VA.

PRICES TO SUIT THE TIMES.

ARCHITECTS.

Anyone contemplating building will find it to their advantage to correspond with R. C. BURKHOLDER & SON before beginning to build. Time, money and trouble saved, by having your plans thoroughly prepared, and the erection superintended by competent architects.

R. C. BURKHOLDER & SON, Architects,

LYNCHBURG, VIRGINIA.

JOHN M. PAYNE,

ATTORNEY-AT-LAW AND COMMISSIONER IN CHANCERY,

OF THE CIRCUIT COURT.

Lynchburg, Virginia.

Practices in the Courts of Lynchburg and neighboring Counties.

J. W. EDWARDS,

PHOTOGRAPHER,

804 Main Street, Lynchburg, Va.

A commodious and thoroughly equipped studio. Pictures taken by the new "Instantaneous Process."

J. PHIL. SHANER,

(LATE OF SHANER BROS.)

Front Stalls Nos. 49 & 50

MARKET HOUSE.

FAMILIES Supplied at Short Notice.

LYNCHBURG, VA.

MOTTO:—QUICK SALES, FAIR DEALINGS AND SMALL PROFITS.

and published in a neat volume, containing also a good deal of valuable extraneous information. The following extracts from the introduction to this work will be found interesting, as bearing directly upon the municipal history of the City:

"The Legislature of Virginia, in October, 1786, vested in certain trustees forty-five acres of the land of John Lynch, 'lying contiguous to Lynch's Ferry,' in the county of Campbell. The village thus laid out was named Lynchburg, after the owner of the soil. The trustees sold this land in half-acre lots, at public auction at first, and subsequently at private sale, for the benefit of John Lynch. The lots brought an average of £50, in the Virginian currency of that day.

RESIDENCE OF MR. JOHN W. FAULKNER.
(ON FIFTH AVENUE.)

"The first meeting of this Board of Trustees was held on the 8th of May, 1787, at which John Clarke, Jesse Burton, Joseph Stratton, William Martin, Micajah Moorman and Achilles Douglas were present. Richard Stith was appointed to survey and lay off the town. According to his map, the eastern boundary of the town was Lynch Street; the western, Court Street; the northern, a line running between Sixth and Seventh Streets, at right angles to Lynch and Court Streets; and the southern, a line running between Eleventh and Twelfth Streets, parallel to the northern boundary.

"The trustees had no control of the town, except over the legal titles of the unsold lots; the money they received for the lots was paid over to John Lynch. They met from time to time from 1786 to 1817.

* * * * * *

"The Town of Lynchburg was first incorporated by an Act of the

HILLSMAN & MYERS,

THE ‡ RELIABLE ‡ CLOTHIERS,

MERCHANT TAILORS AND GENT'S FURNISHERS,

Enjoy an enviable reputation among the Clothing Trade of Central Virginia. Both members are native-born young men, of untiring energy, who by polite attention and fair dealing have gained for themselves a high position as successful merchants. They show one of the largest and best-selected stocks of

Clothing AND Gent's Furnishing Goods

TO BE FOUND IN THE SOUTH.

ARTISTIC ‡ TAILORING ‡ A ‡ SPECIALTY.

903 Main Street, Lynchburg, Va.

WM. H. FORD,

MANUFACTURER OF WAGONS AND BUGGIES, RAILROAD AND FARM CARTS,

Wheelbarrows, Plows, Harrows, Straw Cutters, &c.,

LYNCH STREET, BETWEEN 11TH AND 12TH, LYNCHBURG, VA.

Contractor for all kinds of Stone and Brick Work. Also, constantly on hand in large quantities ALL KINDS OF TERRA COTTA PIPING, for Sewers and Drams, CHIMNEY CAPS, &c.

JOHN W. JONES,

(SUCCESSOR TO ELLIOTT & JONES.)

LIVERY —AND— Sale Stables

911-913 LYNCH STREET, —BETWEEN— 9th and 10th.

Saddle Horses, Hacks and Buggies for Hire. Horses and Mules for Sale.

Carriages, Buggies, Phaetons and Spring Wagons for Hire. ☞ *TELEPHONE* 68.

LYNCHBURG, VA.

General Assembly passed on the 10th of January, 1805. As the Record Book of the Common Council, from its first meeting, in 1805, to the year 1811, has been lost, there is nothing known of the first organization of that body. The first Corporation Court met on the 6th of May, 1805, in the Masonic Hall, situated on the corner of Ninth and Church Streets, which was, for the time, made the Court House for the place.* The Court was held by William Warwick, Mayor; Thomas Wiatt, Recorder; and George D. Winston, Samuel J. Harrison, Roderic Taliaferro and Meredith Lambert, Aldermen. William Norvell was appointed Clerk; Josiah Leake, Commonwealth's Attorney; and John Davis, Sergeant.

"*The First Extension of the Corporate Limits.*—Without additional legislation, John Lynch added several squares to both ends of the Town as laid out in 1786. On the 10th of January, 1805, the Legis-

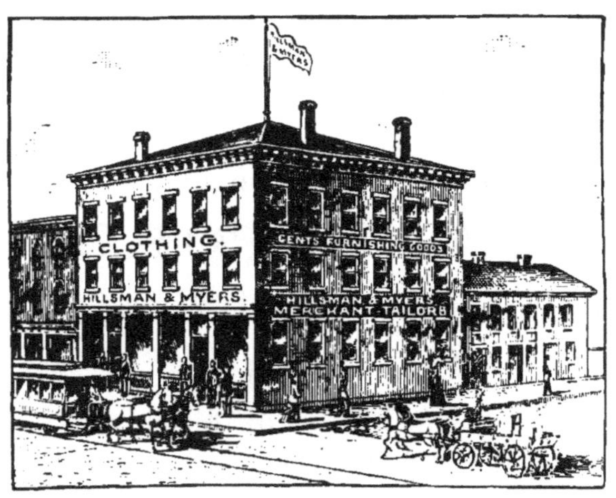

MESSRS. HILLSMAN & MYERS' CLOTHING ESTABLISHMENT.
(NO. 963 MAIN STREET.)

lature passed the 'Act for incorporating the Town of Lynchburg and for enlarging the same.' All half-acre lots of land, as the same were laid off by John Lynch, adjoining the Town of Lynchburg, were declared to be a part of the town as soon as a plat thereof was put on record by John Lynch at Campbell Court House. This was done, and this map, which is still in existence, is the first plat of the town which can be found.

*NOTE.—This Hall, which was a frame building, was removed, on rollers, in 1816, to Fifth Street, between Main and Church Streets, and is now occupied as a residence by Col. Aug. Forsburg, the City Engineer. The present Masonic Hall, was erected in 1816-7, on the site of the old one.—ED.

"*Second Extension.*—On the 9th of February, 1813, the Legislature added to the corporate limits 'that lot of ground conveyed by John Lynch, Sr., to the Corporation of the Town of Lynchburg for a public square, and on which said Corporation hath erected a Court House and Jail.'

* * * * * * * *

"*Fifth Extension.*—On the 30th of January, 1826, the Legislature further extended the limits so as to include the land lying in the following boundaries, to wit:

'Beginning at the east line at the junction of Fifth Street (now Clay) and Sixth Alley (now Twelfth Street); thence along the branch of the south margin of the river to the horse-ford; thence along the banks of the river to Blackwater Creek, and along the creek to the limits of the said town on the north.'

RESIDENCE OF MRS. S. B. McCORKLE.
(CORNER OF MAIN AND PINE STREETS.)

"This Act required that the Hustings Court should appoint three Commissioners, whose duty it should be to lay off the added territory into 'convenient lots, streets and alleys,' and to make a correct plan of the same for recordation. This was done by Thomas Dillard, D. G. Murrell and Ralph Smith, Jr., and their report and plan were duly recorded on the 5th of June, 1827. This is the first extension the limits of which reached the river, and even then the river front was narrow, extending only from the mouth of Blackwater, at the toll-bridge, to the mouth of the Horse-ford at Hurt's Mill.

* * * * * * *

"*Seventh Extension.*—This was the last and most comprehensive. On the 9th day of December, 1870, the Legislature declared that the boundaries of the City of Lynchburg should be extended and defined

Virginian Job Printing House

IMPROVED MACHINERY.

FIRST-CLASS WORK.

1001 MAIN STREET,

LYNCHBURG, - - VIRGINIA,

CHAS. F. & JOS. BUTTON, Proprietors.

Every Kind of Printing Executed in First-Class Style and at Reasonable Prices.

as follows: * * * This act required that a plat of these territories and boundaries 'with the notes and remarks thereon explaining thereof, made by Col. Aug. Forsberg,' the City Engineer, should be certified by the President and Clerk of the Council to the Clerk of the Corporation Court for recordation. It was so certified and has been duly recorded.

"The limits as laid down in this Act are those of the present time. All of these extensions were made without taking the vote of the people thus incorporated.

* * * * * * * *

"Several large districts within the present limits, but outside of the corporate lines of 1827, were laid off into squares and streets by the owners, and the streets so laid off dedicated to the use of the public by placing the plats on record and by other distinct acts declaring such intent.

* * * * * * *

"The first movement towards supplying the town with water was in 1799, when 'The Lynchburg Fire Company' obtained leave from the trustees to sink wells and erect pumps on Main Street for the convenience and safety of the citizens. They availed themselves of the privilege to a very limited extent, although several pumps were placed on the side walks and were used by the public for many years.

"In 1811, the Council granted to John Lynch the privilege of conveying water in wooden pipes through the streets from the springs on his farm at the head of Horseford Branch. These springs still exist on the squares lying between Madison, Federal, Sixth and Seventh; then they were in a secluded forest of original growth For the use of this water Lynch was authorized to charge the citizens, the town reserving the right to use so much of it as was necessary to extinguish fires. The better to avail themselves of this privilege, in 1813 the town authorities built a small reservoir on Ninth Street, between Main and Court, close to the line of Court. This structure was twelve feet square and ten feet deep, and was kept full of water to meet the emergencies of a fire. It seems to have leaked badly, and there was much complaint that the street in its neighborhood was made almost impassable thereby. Four fire plugs were erected at the same time, from which the little fire engine the town then boasted could be supplied. John Lynch sold out his interest in these primitive water works in 1817 to James Wade, and to them alone did our people look for water until 1827, when, after much violent agitation, it was determined by a vote of the people to build a pump house, dam, and the reservoir on Clay Street, at a cost of $50,000. To meet this expense the first debt of the town was created. The reservoir was constructed under the supervision of Albert Stein, Esq., a Civil Engineer of distinction, and was finished in 1830, when it was

JAMES T. WILLIAMS. JEHU R. WILLIAMS. A. S. WHITE. L. G. EFFINGER

JAMES T. WILLIAMS, SON & CO.,

WHOLESALE GROCERS,

JOBBERS OF MANUFACTURED TOBACCO,

And Commission Merchants.

QUOTATIONS GLADLY FURNISHED. CORRESPONDENCE SOLICITED.

608–610 MAIN STREET,

LYNCHBURG, - VIRGINIA.

W. N. BROWN,

—WHOLESALE DEALER IN—

CONFECTIONERIES ∴ AND ∴ FANCY ∴ GROCERIES,

618 MAIN STREET.

LYNCHBURG, - - VIRGINIA.

NO GOODS AT RETAIL.

BUTLER BROS.,

House, Sign and Carriage

PAINTERS,

109 Eleventh Street,

Lynchburg, - - Virginia.

inauguarated amidst great enthusiasm by a very elaborate civic and military procession.

"The reservoir of 1830 seems at the time to have been regarded by our forefathers as large enough to meet the demands of an indefinite future; but the growth of the town, very soon after its completion, developed the need of a further supply.

"Samuel Miller, Esq., who amassed a large fortune in the City of Lynchburg, died on the 2nd of March, 1869. The 22nd clause of his will gave $20,000 to the City 'to be appropriated toward the payment of the debt which may be contracted' in furnishing a future supply of water, provided such supply was furnished within ten years from the day of his death, otherwise the legacy was to lapse. The Council determined to secure the sum to the City, although it was entirely inadequate to the purpose designated in the will; and in May,

RESIDENCE OF MR. JAMES T. WILLIAMS.
(CORNER OF FEDERAL AND NINTH STREETS.)

1877, the construction of the new reservoir on College Hill was commenced and rapidly pushed through, under the control of a committee of citizens, consisting of Wilson P. Bryant, Chairman; C. V. Winfree, Robert Early, John M. Miller and Charles M. Blackford. The plans and specifications were prepared by Col. Aug. Forsberg, the City Engineer, who supervised the work. The contractor was Wm. H. Ford. The work was completed in eighteen months after it was commenced. The present Council is causing a new pump house to be built, in which will be placed new and improved machinery, and it is supposed that these wise outlays will secure to the City a bountiful supply of water for some years to come.

"In 1813 a small structure was erected as a Market House in Ninth or Bridge Street, between Main and Church Streets. Its orig-

THE PEOPLES NATIONAL BANK

—OF—

LYNCHBURG, - - VIRGINIA.

Capital, $205,300. Surplus Fund, $70,000.

C. M. BLACKFORD, *President.* R. W. CRENSHAW, *Vice-President.*
J. W. IVEY, *Cashier.*

DIRECTORS.

C. M. BLACKFORD,	W. W. TYLER,	JACOB H. FRANKLIN,
JOHN D. LANGHORNE,	R. W. CRENSHAW,	T. N. DAVIS,
C. V. WINFREE,	JAMES A. FORD,	JAMES R. GILLIAM.
JOHN H. FLOOD,	JAMES T. WILLIAMS.	

A GENERAL BANKING BUSINESS TRANSACTED.

PARTICULAR ATTENTION GIVEN TO COLLECTIONS.

WEBSTER.

With or without Patent Index.

IT IS THE STANDARD

in the Gov't Printing Office, and Authority with the U. S. Supreme Court, and is recommended by the State Sup'ts of Schools in 36 States.

A Dictionary

118,000 Words, 3000 Engravings,

A Gazetteer of the World

of 25,000 Titles, (recently added) and

A Biographical Dictionary

of nearly 10,000 Noted Persons,

All in One Book.

The latest edition, in the quantity of matter it contains, is believed to be **the largest** volume published. It has **3000** more Words in its vocabulary than are found in any other Am. Dict'y, and nearly 3 times the number of Engravings.

It is an invaluable aid to intelligence in every School and Family.

G. & C. MERRIAM & CO., Pub'rs, Springfield, Mass.

PRICE 50 CENTS.

"HISTORICAL AND INDUSTRIAL GUIDE TO PETERSBURG, VA."

"SKETCH BOOK OF DANVILLE, VA.; ITS MANUFACTURES AND COMMERCE."

"SKETCH BOOK OF PORTSMOUTH, VA.; ITS PEOPLE AND ITS TRADE."

PRICE 30 CENTS.

"SKETCH BOOK OF SUFFOLK, VA.; ITS PEOPLE AND ITS TRADE."

EDWARD POLLOCK,

AUTHOR AND PUBLISHER.

BOX 119, - PORTSMOUTH, VA.

inal cost was $400. This primitive building had additions made to it on several occasions, and when, in 1873, it was finally removed, its proportions, which are still fresh in the memory even of younger citizens, were far from attractive. (See engraving on page 59.)

"The present Market House, on Main Street, was built during the year 1873.

* * * * * * * *

"The first Court House was built in 1812, upon a lot given to the Corporation by John Lynch, Sr. It was taken down and the present structure erected on the same site in 1852.

THE PEOPLES NATIONAL BANK.
(811 MAIN STREET.)

"A census was taken by order of the Council in 1816 by Richardson Taylor, which proved the population of the town to be 3,087, of whom 1,765 were white and 1,322 colored. The census for 1880 shows its population to be 16,012;* but how many are white and how many are colored the books of the new census are not sufficiently closed to ascertain.

"The *Town* of Lynchburg became the CITY of Lynchburg by an Act of the Legislature, on the 20th of May, 1852.

"The first public burying ground was situated at the southwest corner of Court and Tenth Streets. In 1816 it was abandoned, and

*NOTE.—The revised census of 1880 shows the population of the City to have been 15,959 in that year; of these 7,185 were white and 8,171 colored.—ED.

FURNITURE AND MATTRESSES,

A NEW FEATURE.

I have recently made arrangements with some of the largest factories in the United States for the handling of their goods, upon such terms as will enable me to sell their goods at factory prices. When it is remembered that no factory of any importance, or any house in the State, is offering anything like this, I think it well to try me.

In addition to the Jobbing Trade, I propose to continue my Retail Business in all of its branches, and will be glad to serve my old friends, and add as many new ones to my list as possible.

I am now getting out a Catalogue, which I hope to have ready by 1st July. Write for a copy.

J. L. THOMPSON,

THE FURNITURE MAN,

210–212 NINTH STREET, LYNCHBURG, VA.

JACOB SHANER,

Late of Shaner Brothers.

BUTCHER,

AND DEALER IN

LIVE STOCK,

Fresh Meats, &c,

FRONT STALLS

Nos. 1 and 3,

Market House.

RESIDENCE, 1922 GRACE STREET,

Lynchburg, - - Virginia.

FAMILIES AND HOTELS SUPPLIED AT SHORT NOTICE

A. H. PLECKER,

PHOTOGRAPHER,

902 MAIN STREET, LYNCHBURG, VA.

All work promptly and artistically finished. Particular attention given to copying and enlarging old pictures. Also headquarters for Photographic Frames.

the cemetery known as the 'Methodist Grave Yard' became the public cemetery.

"On the 28th of December, 1849, the City contributed $500,000 to the capital stock of the Virginia & Tennessee Railroad Company, partly by direct subscription and partly by a guaranty of six per cent. dividends of the stock to be taken by others.

"On the 18th of February, 1871, it subscribed $200,000 to the capital stock of the Lynchburg & Danville Railroad Company.

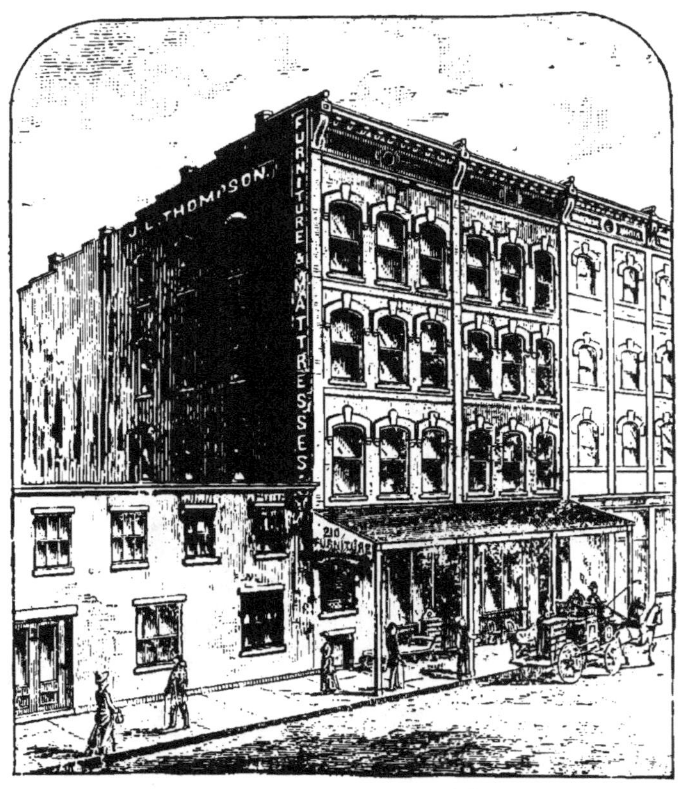

MR. J. L. THOMPSON'S FURNITURE ESTABLISHMENT.
(210 AND 212 NINTH STREET.)

"Without these liberal subscriptions, neither of these great works of internal improvement could at the time have been built.

"On the breaking out of the war, in 1861, Lynchburg furnished very nearly a thousand men as its quota to the Confederate Army, most of whom were equipped at its expense. The number of killed and wounded amongst its citizens was therefore proportionately heavy. No battle took place during the war that the City was not called upon to mourn the loss of its gallant sons.

"The City, though threatened in June, 1864, by Hunter's Army, never was in the hands of the Federal forces until after the surrender at Appomattox Court House, and when it was occupied it was subject to no pillage.

"Since the war, Lynchburg, by reason of the energy, thrift and frugality of its citizens, has overcome many of the obstacles which retarded the prosperity of other Southern towns, and has steadily advanced in population and wealth; and it is now claimed that in the future its progress will be both rapid and sure."

THE FIRST RESERVOIR AND WATER WORKS.

The subjoined is quoted by Mr. Howe, but the authorship is not stated:

"The Lynchburg Water Works, for furnishing the town with an unfailing supply of pure and wholesome water, were constructed in 1828–29, under the direction of Albert Stein, Esq., Engineer, at an expense of $50,000. The height—unprecedented in this country—to which it was necessary to raise the water, renders this one of the most interesting undertakings of the kind in the United States.

"An arm of the James, formed by an island about two miles in length, is crossed, a short distance above the limits of the Corporation, by a dam 10 feet high. A canal of half a mile in length conveys the water to the pump-house on the river bank, at the foot of Third Alley. A double forcing-pump, on the plan of De la Hire, worked by a large breast wheel, impels the water through the ascending pipe, which is 2,000 feet long, to a reservoir containing 400,000 gallons, situated between Fourth and Fifth Streets, and *at the elevation of 253 feet above the level of the river.* Fire-plugs are connected with the distributing pipes at every intersection of the alleys with Second and Third Streets, and afford an admirable security against the danger of fire. The height of the reservoir, above these streets, gives a jet of water, by means of hose pipes, of from 60 to 80 feet elevation, and throws it, in bold and continuous streams, over the roofs of the highest houses.

"The water power created by the dam for the Water Works is amply sufficient for working a large additional amount of machinery, and waits only for a clearer perception by capitalists of the manufacturing advantages of this town, to be brought into extensive use. The cheapness of labor, the abundance of provisions, and the extent and wealth of the country looking this way for supplies of domestic, as well as of foreign goods, unite with the vast water-power, actually prepared and ready for any application, in inviting the attention of men of capital and enterprise to this important subject."

The following account of the ceremony of laying the corner stone of the Water Works is from a local newspaper of that date:

"INTERESTING EVENT.—On Saturday last, (August 23rd, 1828,) an event deeply interesting to Lynchburg took place; one in which the convenience, health and safety of us all are involved. The corner stone of the Lynchburg Water Works was laid—works, the mag-

MESSRS. WITT & WATKINS' BOOT AND SHOE WAREHOUSE.
(MAIN STREET, BETWEEN EIGHTH AND NINTH.)

nitude of which exceeds any ever attempted in Virginia. . . . The stone was laid with civic, masonic and military ceremonies. About 9 A. M. the procession was formed at the Presbyterian Church, at the lower end of Main Street, in the following order: The Military; the reverend Clergy; the Engineer; the members of the Common Council, preceded by the Water Committee; the Judge of the General Court for the Circuit and Mayor of the Corporation; the Recorder and Aldermen; the Masonic Fraternity; Citizens.

"When the procession, under the directions of the Marshals of the day,—Major James B. Risque, Col. Maurice H. Langhorne, and Captains R. R. Phelps, Samuel I. Wiat, and A. M. Gilliam—reached the ground, the Artillery and Rifle Companies formed a hollow square, within which were the Masons, the adjacent banks being thronged with spectators.

"The impressive ceremonies commenced with a prayer, appropriate to the occasion, by the Rev. W. S. Reid, followed by solemn music. The Rev. F. G. Smith then implored of the Supreme Architect of the Universe a blessing on the undertaking. The Masonic Fraternity proceeded to lay the corner stone; the plate bears the following inscription:

> This stone, the foundation of a work executed by order of the Common Council of Lynchburg, for supplying the town with water, was laid under the direction of John Victor, John Thurman, John Early, David G. Murrell, and Samuel Claytor, by the Rt. W. Howson S. White, D. D., G. Master, and the Worshipful Maurice H. Garland, M. of Marshall Lodge, No. 39, of Free and Accepted Masons, on the 23d August, A. M. 5828, A. D. 1828, in presence of the Mayor, Recorder, Aldermen and Common Councilmen of said Town; the members of said Lodge; the Artillery and Rifle Companies, commanded by Captains J. E. Norvell and James W. Pegram, and numerous Citizens, Albon McDaniel, Esq., Mayor, John Thurman, Esq., President of the Council, Albert Stein, Esq., Engineer.

"Mr. John Victor, Chairman of the Water Committee, delivered an address, after which the military fired a salute, and the gratified beholders returned to their homes, all, we hope, determined to use their efforts to carry on the work to a successful termination. We cordially unite with Mr. Victor in saying: 'Let us join hands, nothing doubting that we, too, can accomplish what others have so often done.'"

THE JAMES RIVER AND KANAWHA CANAL.

This great highway, which was projected about the year 1842, was for many years the chief, if not the only means of transportation enjoyed by Lynchburg, and formed its principal avenue of communication with the outside world. It extended from Richmond, along the margin of the James River, two hundred miles, through the centre of the State, to a point near the base of the Alleghany Mountains. This

Canal afforded a convenient route between the Western States and the Atlantic Ocean, and was expected by its projectors to become the great thoroughfare of the Continent. A survey of its proposed extensions was made by officers of the United States Engineer Department, and a full and favorable report submitted to Congress. It was hoped that the National Gcvernment would undertake the completion and enlargement of the Canal, which would then have afforded uninterrupted water communication between the Mississippi and Missouri Rivers and their tributaries, and the Atlantic Ocean at Hampton Roads. But, alas for such primitive enterprises in this age of steam and electricity! The James River and Kanawha Canal. which gave long and faithful service to the State during its lifetime, and from which so much was expected during the after years which never came, is now a mere memory of departed utility—its bed dry and in many places overgrown with grass and weeds, and its tow-path, once the familiar treadmill of the patient horse and mule, now converted into the road-bed of the Richmond and Alleghany Railroad.

THE LYNCHBURG FEMALE ORPHAN ASYLUM.

THE PORTER'S LODGE.

This beneficent institution, for the education and support of white female orphans, owes its existence to the philanthropy of the late Samuel Miller, a native of Albemarle County, Virginia, who was born in the year 1792. It is one of the noblest monuments to personal benevolence and generosity to be found in this or any other of the Southern States. The parentage of the founder was obscure, and his early years were passed in poverty. Having neither social nor scholastic advatages, he succeeded, by sheer hard work and steady application, in acquiring, without a teacher other than his own practical intelligence, a fair education, which proved of infinite value throughout his long and prosperous life. In early manhood he settled in Lynchburg, engaged in mercantile pursuits, and eventually amassed an enormous fortune, estimated at several millions of dollars. For many years before his death, which occurred in 1869, he retired, owing to impaired heatlh, to his estate in the country, about six miles from

Lynchburg, where he was still a hard worker, being interested in extensive speculations in railroad and other securities, in every section of the country.

Although a bachelor, Mr. Miller had, for a long period, cherished a scheme for the establishment, at or near Lynchburg, of an Asylum for the maintenance and training of the female orphans of the City and its vicinity. As early as 1849, he procured the passage, by the General Assembly, of an Act of Incorporation, embodying the ideas he then entertained on that subject; but it was not until 1868—the year preceding his death—that he engaged actively in formulating and maturing his plans, with a view to the early establishment of the institution.

In June, 1868, Mr. Miller appointed as incorporators Ambrose B. Rucker, John G. Meem, George D. Davis, John H. Flood, Lorenzo Norvell, Charles W. Button, Don P. Halsey, J. J. Terrill, David E. Spence, William A. Miller, John F. Slaughter, Thomas E. Murrell and James O. Williams, to take charge of the real estate—a beautiful grove covering about forty acres, near the southwestern boundary of the City—that he had reserved for this purpose, and to assume custody of the bonds that he had appropriated to the endowment of the Asylum, with authority to erect the necessary buildings and to assume the management of the institution. The first meeting of these gentlemen—to formally accept the trust—was held on the 10th of June, 1868, and on the following day a new charter was granted by the Circuit Court of Lynchburg, Mr. Ambrose B. Rucker having been elected the first President of the Asylum.

In November, 1869, a committee, consisting of John G. Meem, Charles W. Button and George D. Davis, was appointed to select plans for the building, and, in pursuance of that object, visited various similar establishments in northern cities to ascertain the most approved methods of heating, ventilation, &c. They finally adopted, in the main, the plan of the hospital presided over by the late Dr. Muhlenburg, in New York.

On the 12th of July, 1870, the site was chosen by the Directors, and in due time the Lynchburg Female Orphan Asylum, as it now exists, became an accomplished fact, at a cost of about $90,000. The addition of the beautiful porter's lodge was made in 1881, at a further cost of $5,750.

THE LYNCHBURG FEMALE ORPHAN ASYLUM.

Contiguous lands have been purchased from time to time, and the enclosure now contains about seventy-five acres. These grounds the Directors have reclaimed and improved year by year, and they are now among the most picturesque and park-like in the State.

The remains of the benevolent founder, who died on March 27th, 1869, have been entombed within the grounds, beneath a graceful granite shaft—said to be the largest single shaft ever quarried in the United States—which was erected to his memory at a cost of $5,250. The endowment that came from Mr. Miller during his lifetime, and from his estate after his decease—apart from the land he presented—amounts to about $325,000.

Sixty-two orphan girls are now supported wholly at this Asylum, while at the same time they are being carefully educated, as well as instructed and exercised in the practical affairs of domestic life. During all the years that the Asylum has been in occupation, only one death—that of a little child—has occurred there.

In the chapel hangs a life-size portrait of Mr Miller, painted by F. J. Fisher, the now famous artist, of Washington. As a work of art it is unsurpassed in its fine execution and its fidelity to life; while it may also be regarded as a veritable art curiosity, inasmuch as it was painted entirely from memory, after a lapse of ten years since the artist and his subject had met. Those who were most intimate with Mr. Miller during his later years have pronounced the picture a perfect portrait. It was finished in 1881, and purchased for $2,000.

The Corporation, at the date of this publication—1887—is constituted as follows: *President*, John H. Flood, who has served continuously since April 2nd, 1872; *Vice-President*, William A. Miller; *Directors*, John H. Flood, William A. Miller, John F. Slaughter, Charles W. Button, William A. Strother, David E. Spence, Thomas E. Murrell, J. J. Terrill, John W. Carroll, James M. Booker, Charles W. Statham, Thomas D. Davis and Robert T. Craighill; *Secretary and Treasurer*, A. W. Talley; *Matron*, Mrs. E. J. Britton; *Teachers*, Miss R. Cary Williams and Miss Mildred A. Harris.

THE WAR BETWEEN THE STATES.

With the events of this cruel and unnatural conflict, which, after four terrible years of unequalled heroism and voluntary self-sacrifice on the part of her noble sons and daughters, resulted in the overthrow and humiliation of the Southern Confederacy, this narrative

THE LYNCHBURG IRON COMPANY'S BLAST FURNACE.

E. BURD GRUBB, *President.* ED. S. HUTTER, *Manager.*
A. VAN RENSSELAER, *Vice-President.* A. FULLARTON, *Sec'ty and Treasr.*

The Lynchburg Blast Furnace is owned by The Lynchburg Iron Company, and was built in 1881, by General E. Burd Grubb, who owns most of the stock.

The Furnace is located between the James River and the main line of the Richmond & Alleghany Railroad, within the City limits. Its Stack House and Iron Yard are reached by the Va. Midland and Norfolk & Western Railroads, as well as by the Richmond & Alleghany.

The Company's land fronts about 2,000 ft. on the R. & A. with a width of about 300 feet to the River, and a water power right of about 200 horse-power.

The capacity of the Stack is 45 tons pig iron per day, or 14,000 tons per year.

Two-thirds of the ore used is mined at Blue Ridge Mines, (brown hemitite) of fine quality, and the other one third, the neutral magnetic ores, from Lower James River and from Pittsylvania County.

The Iron made is mainly a fine quality of Foundry Iron, soft and fluid, and is sold at full prices as fast as made.

The Furnace, and the mines which supply the material, give employment to about 200 men. The annual freights paid amount to about $100,000.

General Grubb, the President of the Company, is a gentlemen of large fortune, liberal and progressive in his views, and was one of the first capitalists from the North to invest largely in Virginia Iron Works. He is the owner of the Blue Ridge Iron Mines, 11 miles west of Lynchburg, on the N. & W. R. R., and connected with the latter by a branch road two miles long. These mines probably contain the largest deposit of hemitite ores yet opened or worked in Virginia.

The Blast Furnace, the various mines and all the affairs of the Company in Virginia are under the management of Maj. Ed. S. Hutter, a Virginian and a native of this City.

has very little concern; for Lynchburg, more blest than many of her sister cities of Virginia, was providentially spared the horrors of a siege, or even of a single battle, although for many months she was fortified, and presented all the characteristics of a military camp. Especially was this the case in the latter part of 1863, when Sheridan's cavalry were expected to visit the city, and the latter prepared herself to give them a warm reception. From time to time, too, captured Federal soldiers found temporary quarters here, *en route* to the regular prisons.

Besides the Home Guard, the only military organization of that day still surviving, which was mustered into the State service on April

THE LYNCHBURG IRON COMPANY'S BLAST FURNACE.

24th, 1861, and did gallant service throughout the continuance of hostilities, Lynchburg furnished nearly a thousand good and true soldiers as her quota to the Confederate armies, and her loss was therefore proportionately heavy. Scarce a battle was fought which did not bring bereavement to at least one household in the City—bereavement which was to some extent softened by the knowledge that the mourned one had died gallantly in the discharge of his duty and in the defense of his honor and his home.

The principal event of the war, so far as Lynchburg was immediately concerned, occurred in the summer of 1864, when the Federal troops under General Hunter advanced upon the City in force,

RUCKER & BARNETT,

Leaf Tobacco Commission Merchants.

The firm above named is a representative one in this important branch of the tobacco business. The senior partner, Mr. S. B. Rucker, has been connected with the trade in Lynchburg since 1869, and Mr. J. T. Barnett has had twelve years' experience in his present field of labor. Their copartnership was formed three years ago and their entire attention is given to the sale of leaf tobacco. Messrs. RUCKER & BARNETT are widely known and enjoy the confidence of planters throughout a large section of Virginia. In 1886 they sold on commission 6,000,000 lbs. of tobacco at the several public warehouses of Lynchburg. They are always well informed regarding the condition of the Tobacco Market and the prices which can be realized, and give their earnest, individual efforts to secure and promote by every honorable and legitimate means the best interests of their principals. They have no dealings of a private nature which might conflict with those of their customers, and do not engage in transactions of a speculative character. By activity, prudence and enterprise, their reputation has become thoroughly established as systematic and prompt business men. All planters and persons who ship tobacco to them may feel confident that sales will be made at the highest obtainable prices, and prompt returns rendered.

EXCELSIOR LIVERY & SALE STABLES,

NO. 916 LYNCH STREET,

IS THE PLACE TO GO FOR THE MOST STYLISH

RIDING AND DRIVING HORSES,

—FOR THE NEWEST AND MOST ELEGANT—

LANDAUS, ‡ PHÆTONS, ‡ SURRIES, ‡ &C.

Our Livery is unsurpassed by any in the State. Our Stable has been pronounced by the leading Physician of our place to be the BEST VENTILATED AND HEALTHIEST IN THE CITY.

STRICTEST ATTENTION GIVEN STOCK COMMITTED TO OUR CARE. SPECIAL ATTENTION GIVEN TO THE PURCHASE AND SALE OF HORSES AND MULES.

ELLIOTT & DOSS, PROPRIETORS.

Telephone Call No. 16. 916 LYNCH STREET, LYNCHBURG, VA.

with instructions to capture and occupy it. The circumstances under which his plans were frustrated are thus related in "A Memoir of the Last Year of the War of Independence in the Confederate States of America," by Lieut. Gen. Jubal A. Early, published in 1867—the foot-notes as well as the text being his own:

"MARCH TO LYNCHBURG, AND PURSUIT OF HUNTER.

"On the 12th of June, 1864, while the 2nd Corps (Ewell's) of the Army of Northern Virginia was lying near Gaines' Mill, in rear of

"CITY VIEW," ON AMHERST HEIGHTS: OVERLOOKING THE CITY. RESIDENCE OF MR. SAMUEL B. RUCKER.

Hill's line at Cold Harbour, I received verbal orders from General Lee to hold the corps, with two of the battalions of artillery attached to it, in readiness to move to the Shenandoah Valley. Nelson's and Braxton's battalions were selected, and Brigadier-General Long was ordered to accompany me as Chief of Artillery. After dark, on the same day, written instructions were given me by General Lee, by which I was directed to move, with the force designated, at 3 o'clock next morning, for the Valley, by way of Louisa C. H. and Charlottesville, and through Brown's or Swift Run Gap in the Blue Ridge, as I might find most advisable; to strike Hunter's force in the rear, and, if possible, destroy it; then to move down the Valley, cross the Potomac near Leesburg in Loudoun County, or at or above Harper's Ferry, as I might find most practicable, and threaten Washington City. I was further directed to communicate with General Breckenridge, who would co-operate with me in the attack on Hunter, and the expedition into Maryland.

"At this time the railroad and telegraph lines between Charlottesville and Lynchburg had been cut by a cavalry force from Hunter's army; and those between Richmond and Charlottesville had been cut by Sheridan's cavalry, from Grant's army; so that there was no communication with Breckenridge. Hunter was supposed to be at Staunton with his whole force, and Breckenridge was supposed to be at Waynesboro, or Rockfish Gap. If such had been the case, the route designated by General Lee would have carried me into the Valley in Hunter's rear.

"The 2nd Corps now numbered a little over 8,000 muskets for duty. It had been on active and arduous service in the field for forty days, and had been engaged in all the great battles from the Wilderness to Cold Harbour, sustaining very heavy losses at Spotsylvania C. H. where it lost nearly an entire division, including its commander, Major-General Johnson, who was made prisoner. Of the Brigadier-Generals with it at the commencement of the campaign, only one remained in command of his brigade. Two (Gordon and Ramseur) had been made Major-Generals; one (G. H. Steuart) had been captured; four (Pegram, Hays, J. A. Walker, and R. D. Johnston) had been severely wounded; and four (Stafford, J. M. Jones, Daniel, and Doles) had been killed in action. Constant exposure to the weather, a limited supply of provisions, and two weeks' service in the swamps north of the Chickahominy had told on the health of the men. Divisions were not stronger than brigades ought to have been, nor brigades than regiments.

"On the morning of the 13th, at 2 o'clock, we commenced the march; and, on the 16th, arrived at the Rivanna River, near Charlottesville, having marched over eighty miles in four days.*

"From Louisa C. H. I had sent a dispatch to Gordonsville, to be forwarded, by telegraph, to Breckenridge; and, on my arrival at

*On the 15th, we passed over the ground, near Trevillian's depot, on which Hampton and Sheridan had fought, on the 11th and 12th Hampton had defeated Sheridan, and was then in pursuit of him. Grant claims, in his report, that, on the 11th, Sheridan drove our cavalry "from the field, in complete rout;" and says, when he advanced towards Gordonsville, on the 12th, "he found the enemy reinforced by infantry, behind well-constructed rifle-pits, about five miles from the latter place, and too strong to successfully assault."

This is as thoroughly a fancy sketch as can well be manufactured. There was not an infantry soldier in arms nearer the scene of action than with General Lee's army, near Cold Harbour; and the "well-constructed rifle-pits" were nothing more than rails put up in the manner in which cavalry were accustomed to arrange them to prevent a charge. Sheridan mistook some of Hampton's cavalry, dismounted and fighting on foot, for infantry; and the statement was made to cover his defeat.

Charlottesville, on the 16th, to which place I rode in advance of the troops, I received a telegram from him, dated at Lynchburg, informing me that Hunter was then in Bedford county, about twenty miles from that place, and moving on it.

"The railroad and telegraph between Charlottesville and Lynchburg had been, fortunately, but slightly injured by the enemy's cavalry, and had been repaired. The distance between the two places was sixty miles, and there were no trains at Charlottesville, except one which belonged to the Central road, and was about starting for Waynesboro. I ordered this to be detained, and immediately directed, by telegram, all the trains of the two roads to be sent to me with all dispatch, for the purpose of transporting my troops to Lynchburg. The trains were not in readiness to take the troops on board

RESIDENCE OF MR. W. H. WREN.
(COURT STREET, BETWEEN TENTH AND ELEVENTH.)

until sunrise on the morning of the 17th, and then only enough were furnished to transport about half my infantry. Ramseur's division, one brigade of Gordon's division, and part of another were put on the trains, as soon as they were ready, and started for Lynchburg. Rodes' division and the residue of Gordon's were ordered to move along the railroad, to meet the trains on their return. The artillery and wagon trains had been started on the ordinary roads at daylight.

"I accompanied Ramseur's division, going on the front train, but the road and rolling stock were in such bad condition that I did not reach Lynchburg until about 1 o'clock in the afternoon, and the other trains were much later. I found General Breckenridge in bed, suffering from an injury received by the fall of a horse killed under him in action near Cold Harbour. He had moved from Rockfish

LYNCHBURG FERTILIZER COMPANY.

MESSRS. WRIGHT & CRAIGHILL, Manufacturers and Proprietors of THE LYNCHBURG FERTILIZER AND INSECTICIDE, have, within the past two years, originated an enterprise which has already attracted wide-spread attention, and is destined to become in the near future one of the gigantic and overshadowing interests in the commercial and agricultural history and material progress of Virginia and the United States. It bids fair to be one of those astonishing outgrowths of American industry and inventive genius, which are constantly springing up and exciting the admiration of mankind.

The lands of the older States of the Atlantic Seaboard have become impoverished by unskilled cultivation and the excessive use of stimulating guanos; and the planters of the South have been so remorselessly victimized by the fraudulent fertilizers which flood the market, that the agricultural depression of that once teeming region is melancholy to witness. Moreover, the insects, (bred and nourished by the filthy manures manufactured of decayed vegetable and animal matter), have become nearly as destructive to growing vegetation as the locusts of Egypt. All over the country, indeed, whilst the staple crops of all kinds have received and are receiving incalculable damage, the cultivation of many of the most useful vegetables, luscious fruits and beautiful flowers has become nearly extinct, by reason of the animal parasites which feed upon the tender plants and prevent their perfection and fruitage; and it has really come to pass that no vegetation whatever, from the forest oak or standard fruit tree to the products of the farm, the garden and the hot house, is exempt from the blighting curse.

In this deplorable condition of affairs the enterprizing firm of Wright & Craighill have put upon the market their Lynchburg Fertilizer and Insecticide—an article of merchandize whose formula and preparation have taxed the highest chemical talent of this Country and Europe, resulting in the happy combination of *a perfect fertilizer* and *a perfect insecticide*, adapted to all crops, soils and climates. This valuable preparation does not *stimulate* but *feeds* the soil, whilst gently stimulating the growing crops and preventing the hurtful interference of insects with its healthy growth.

It is not the province of the historian to deal too much in details, but rather to contemplate the wider field of human demand and supply in the complex and ever-varying interests of communities in Towns and Cities, States and Nations; and in this connection it may be averred as a rational belief that no device or invention has ever originated in this or any country more promising than THE LYNCHBURG FERTILIZER AND INSECTICIDE for the producer and consumer of vegetable food, or better calculated to clothe the earth with charming verdure and fill it with the beauty and fragrance of blooming flowers.

Gap to Lynchburg by a forced march, as soon as Hunter's movement towards that place was discovered. When I showed him my instructions, he very readily and cordially offered to co-operate with me, and serve under my command.

"Hunter's advance from Staunton had been impeded by a brigade of cavalry, under Brigadier-General McCausland, which had been managed with great skill, and kept in his front all the way, and he was reported to be then advancing on the old stone turnpike from Liberty, in Bedford County, by New London, and watched by Imboden with a small force of cavalry.

"As General Breckenridge was unable to go out, at his request, General D. H. Hill, who happened to be in town, had made arrangements for the defense of the city, with such troops as were at hand. Brigadier-General Hays, who was an invalid from a wound received at Spotsylvania Court House, had tendered his services and also aided in making arrangements for the defense. I rode out with General Hill to examine the line selected by him, and make a reconnoisance of the country in front. Slight works had been hastily thrown up on College Hill, covering the turnpike and Forest roads from Liberty, which were manned by Breckenridge's infantry and the dismounted cavalry of the command which had been with Jones at Piedmont. The reserves, invalids from the hospitals, and the cadets from the Military Institute at Lexington, occupied other parts of the line. An inspection satisfied me that, while this arrangement was the best which could be made under the circumstances in which General Hill found himself, yet it would leave the town exposed to the fire of the enemy's artillery, should he advance to the attack, and I therefore determined to meet the enemy with my troops in front.

"We found Imboden about four miles out on the turnpike, near an old Quaker church, to which position he had been gradually forced back by the enemy's infantry. My troops, as they arrived, had been ordered in front of the works to bivouac, and I immediately sent orders for them to move out on this road, and two brigades of Ramseur's division arrived just in time to be thrown across the road, at a redoubt about two miles from the city, as Imboden's command was driven back by vastly superior numbers. These brigades, with two pieces of artillery in the redoubt, arrested the progress of the enemy, and Ramseur's other brigade, and the part of Gordon's divison which had arrived, took position on the same line. The enemy opened a heavy fire of artillery on us, but, as night soon came on, he went into camp in our front.

"On my arrival at Lynchburg, orders had been given for the immediate return of the trains for the rest of my infantry, and I expected it to arrive by the morning of the 18th, but it did not get to Lynchburg until late in the afternoon of that day. Hunter's force was considerably larger than mine would have been, had it all been

THE LYNCHBURG FURNITURE CO.,

WHOLESALE AND RETAIL FURNITURE DEALERS.

This house commenced business in May, 1885, and from the start success has attended its operations.

The members of the firm are W. P. Dillon, C. W. Liggan, and Gilliam & Co. The two first, who are enterprising and energetic young business men, give their constant and persevering attention to the management of the Company's business, (Gilliam & Co. having a pecuniary interest alone.)

Stock purchases are made direct from the manufacturers on the most advantageous terms, and, being content to sell goods on a reasonable margin of profit, the Company has, through close and polite attention to the wants of their customers, established in a comparatively short space of time an entensive and ever-increasing trade.

Their warerooms contain a large and varied assortment of all kinds of Furniture, suited to every taste and every purse. They also carry a large and diversified line of Mattresses.

Their present business premises are at **917 Main Street,** but about July 1st they will remove to the commodious four-story brick, iron-front building now being erected for them at **1023 Main Street,** a cut of which appears in the opposite page. The new building is 125 feet in length, and will be one of the largest, most ornate and complete business blocks in the City of Lynchburg.

JOHN T. EDWARDS,

—AGENT—

LYNCHBURG, VA.

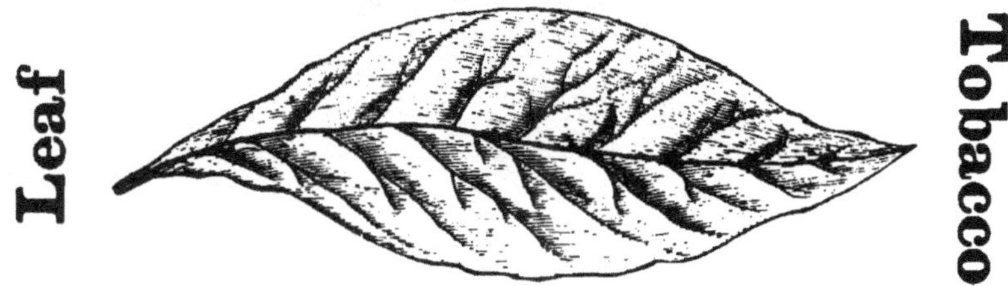

Broker and Commission Merchant.

Consignments of all kinds of Leaf Tobacco solicited. Special attention given to the sale of Prized Leaf Tobacco. Dealers will find it to their interest to send me their Tobacco or guaranteed samples for sale. I keep a full line of all classes of Virginia and North Carolina Tobacco.

Burley Tobacco a Specialty,

The attention of buyers is invited to my stock. Correspondence Solicited.

up, and as it was of the utmost consequence to the army at Richmond that he should not get into Lynchburg, I did not feel justified in attacking him until I could do so with a fair prospect of success.* I contented myself, therefore, with acting on the defensive on the 18th, throwing Breckenridge's infantry and a part of his artillery on the front line, while that adopted by General Hill was occupied by the dismounted cavalry and the irregular troops. During the day, there was artillery firing and skirmishing along the line, and, in the afternoon, an attack was made on our line, to the right of the turn-

NEW BUILDING OF THE LYNCHBURG FURNITURE COMPANY.
(MAIN STREET, BETWEEN TENTH AND ELEVENTH.)

pike, which was handsomely repulsed with considerable loss to the enemy. A demonstration of the enemy's cavalry on the Forest road, was checked by part of Breckenridge's infantry under Wharton, and McCausland's cavalry.

"On the arrival of the cars from Richmond this day, Major-Generals Elzey and Ransom reported for duty, the former to command

*From the best information I have received, I am satisfied Hunter's force exceeded 30,000 men.

the infantry and dismounted cavalry of Breckenridge's command, and the latter to command the cavalry. The mounted cavalry consisted of the remnants of several brigades divided into two commands, one under Imboden, and the other under McCausland. It was badly mounted and armed, and its efficiency much impaired by the defeat at Piedmont, and the arduous service it had recently gone through.

As soon as the remainder of my infantry arrived by the railroad, though none of my artillery had gotten up, arrangements were made for attacking Hunter at daylight on the 19th, but, sometime after midnight, it was discovered that he was moving, though it was not

MR. H. SILVERTHORN'S JEWELRY STORE.
(912 MAIN STREET.)

known whether he was retreating, or moving so as to attack Lynchburg on the south where it was vulnerable, or to attempt to join Grant on the south side of James River. Pursuit could not, therefore, be made at once, as a mistake, if either of the last two objects had been contemplated, would have been fatal. At light, however, the pursuit commenced, the 2nd Corps moving along the turnpike, over which it was discovered Hunter was retreating, and Elzey's command on the right, along the Forest road, while Ransom was ordered to move on the right of Elzey, with McCausland's cavalry, and endeavor to strike the enemy at Liberty or the Peaks of Otter. Imboden, who was on the road from Lynchburg to Campbell Court House, to watch a body of the enemy's cavalry, which had moved in that direction the day before, was to have moved on the left towards Liberty, but orders did not reach him in time. The enemy's rear was overtaken at Liberty, twenty-five miles from Lynchburg, just before night, and driven through that place, after a brisk skirmish, by Ramseur's division. The day's march on the old turnpike, which was very rough, had been terrible. McCausland had taken the wrong road and did not reach Liberty until after the enemy had been driven through the town.

"It was here ascertained that Hunter had not retreated on the route by the Peaks of Otter, over which he had advanced, but had taken the road to Buford's depot, at the foot of the Blue Ridge, which would enable him to go either by Salem, Fincastle, or Buchanan. Ransom was, therefore, ordered to take the route, next day, by the Peaks of Otter, and endeavor to intercept the enemy should he move by Buchanan or Fincastle. The pursuit was resumed early on the morning of the 20th, and on our arrival in sight of Buford's, the enemy's rear guard was seen going into the mountain on the road towards Salem. As this left the road to Buchanan open, my aide, Lieutenant Pitzer, was sent across the mountain to that place, with orders to Ransom to move for Salem. Lieutenant Pitzer was also instructed to ride all night and send directions, by courier from Fincastle, and telegraph from Salem, to have the road through the mountains to Lewisburg and South-Western Virginia blockaded. The enemy was pursued into the mountains at Buford's Gap, but he had taken possession of the crest of the Blue Ridge, and put batteries in position commanding a gorge, through which the road passes, where it was impossible for a regiment to move in line. I had endeavored to ascertain if there was not another way across the mountain by which I could get around the enemy, but all the men, except the old ones, had gotten out of the way, and the latter, as well as the women and children, were in such a state of distress and alarm, that no reliable information could be obtained from them. We tried to throw forces up the sides of the mountains to get at the enemy, but they were so rugged that night came on before anything could be accomplished, and we had to desist, though not until a very late hour in the night.

"By a mistake of the messenger, who was sent with orders to General Rodes, who was to be in the lead next morning, there was some delay in his movement on the 21st, but the pursuit was resumed very shortly after sun-rise. At the Big Lick, it was ascertained that the enemy had turned off from Salem towards Lewisburg on a road which passes through the mountains at a narrow pass called the

'Hanging Rock,' and my column was immediately turned towards that point, but on arriving there it was ascertained that the enemy's rear guard had passed through the gorge. McCausland had struck his column at this point and captured ten pieces of artillery, some wagons, and a number of prisoners; but, the enemy having brought up a heavy force, McCausland was compelled to fall back, carrying off, however, the prisoners, and a part of the artillery, and disabling the rest so that it could not be removed. As the enemy had got into the mountains, where nothing useful could be accomplished by pursuit, I did not deem it proper to continue it farther. A great part of my command had had nothing to eat for the last two days, except a little bacon which was obtained at Liberty. The cooking utensils were in the trains, and the effort to have bread baked at Lynchburg

CITY RESERVOIRS AND CHURCH (R. C.) OF THE HOLY CROSS.
(CORNER OF CLAY AND SEVENTH STREETS.)

had failed. Neither the wagon trains, nor the artillery of the 2nd Corps, were up, and I knew that the country through which Hunter's route led for forty or fifty miles, was, for the most part, a desolate mountain region; and that his troops were taking everything in the way of provisions and forage which they could lay their hands on. My field officers, except those of Breckenridge's command, were on foot, as their horses could not be transported on the trains from Charlottesville. I had seen our soldiers endure a great deal, but there was a limit to the endurance even of Confederate soldiers. A stern chase of infantry is a very difficult one, and Hunter's men were marching for their lives, his disabled being carried in his provision train which was now empty. My cavalry was not strong

LYNCHBURG MARBLE AND GRANITE WORKS,

821–827 Church Street, Corner of Ninth Street,

J. I. VAN NESS, Proprietor.

This establishment, which has in a marked manner for many years enjoyed the favor of the public, keeps up with the times in quality, variety and prices of its productions.

The fact of its having so successfully overcome competition is sufficient endorsement of its past methods of conducting business, and should be a guarantee for the future.

We undertake country work of every kind and size, including Marble and Granite Monuments and Headstones, Iron Railings, Vaults, Marble, Limestone and Granite Curbing, Building Marble, &c.

A visit to our shops will convince the customer that he can obtain more for his money, in quality of material and beauty of workmanship than most cities offer, and with a large assortment of designs from which to select, his taste can be gratified in every particular.

We obtain low rates of freight which are guaranteed the customer.

Thankful for past patronage we solicit a continuance of the same, promising satisfaction in every respect.

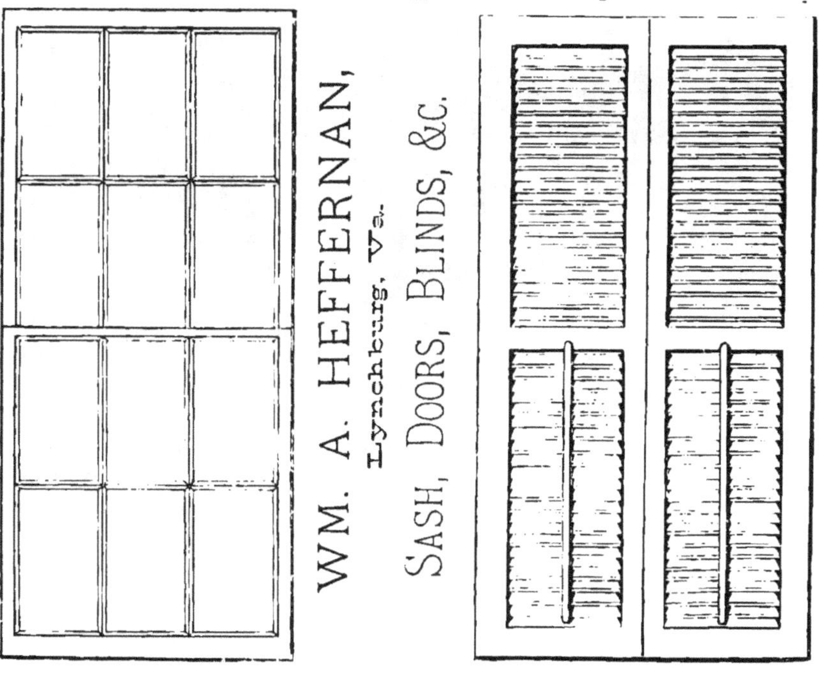

enough to accomplish anything of importance, and a further pursuit could only have resulted in disaster to my command from want of provisions and forage.

"I was glad to see Hunter take the route to Lewisburg, as I knew he could not stop short of the Kanawha River, and he was, therefore, disposed of for some time. Had he moved to South-Western

LYNCHBURG MARBLE AND GRANITE WORKS—J. I. VAN NESS, PROP'R.
(CHURCH STREET—FOOT OF COURT HOUSE HILL.)

Virginia he would have done us incalculable mischief, as there were no troops of any consequence in that quarter, but plenty of supplies at that time. I should, therefore, have been compelled to follow him.*

*Grant, in his report says: "General Hunter, owing to a want of ammunition to give battle, retired from before the place," (Lynchburg). This is a little remarkable, as it appears that this expedition had been long contemplated and was one of the prominent features of the campaign of 1864. Sheridan, with his cavalry, was to have united with Hunter at Lynchburg, and the two together were to have destroyed General Lee's communications and depots of supplies, and then have joined Grant. Can it be believed that Hunter set out on so important an expedition with an insufficient supply of ammu.

"My command had marched sixty miles, in the three days pursuit, over very rough roads, and that part of it from the Army of Northern Virginia had had no rest since leaving Gaines' Mill. I determined, therefore, to rest on the 22nd, so as to enable the wagons and artillery to get up, and prepare the men for the long march before them. Imboden had come up, following on the road through Salem after the enemy, and the cavalry was sent through Fincastle, to watch the enemy and annoy him as he passed through the mountains towards Lewisburg, and also ascertain whether he would endeavor to get into the Valley towards Lexington or Staunton."

RESTORED PEACE.

During the twenty years which have elapsed since the close of the war and the unsettled state of affairs—national and municipal—which necessarily supervened, no startling events have occurred whereby the even course of Lynchburg's development has been disturbed. Indeed her subsequent history may be written in a very few comprehensive words—Peace and Plenty, Prosperity and Progress. In all matters affecting her commercial interests she has been vigilant, enterprising and aggressive, until her wealth, in proportion to her population, is exceeded by that of only one other city in the United States. Valuable and permanent public improvements have been the mile-stones which have recorded the flight of the passing years, while private enterprise has been actively and successfully employed in establishing the beautiful "Hill City" as one of the leading Business Centres of the South. Her great natural advantages have been enhanced and utilized in various ways, but there is still room for the profitable investment of much capital in any of the numerous manufacturing and mercantile pursuits for which this locality is so eminently adapted. That the community is fully alive to the value of its own possessions in this respect is evidenced by the fact that several new and important industries have been inaugurated here, within the past few years, by resident capitalists, and others, of greater magnitude, may be looked for almost immediately.

---

nition? He had fought only the battle of Piedmont, with a part of his force, and it was not a very severe one, as Jones' force was a small one and composed mostly of cavalry. Crook's column not being there was not engaged. Had Sheridan defeated Hampton at Trevillian's, he would have reached Lynchburg after destroying the railroad on the way, and I could not have reached there in time to do any good. But Hampton defeated Sheridan, and the latter saw "infantry" "too strong to successfully assault." Had Hunter moved on Lynchburg, with energy, that place would have fallen before it was possible for me to get there. But he tarried on the way for purposes which will hereafter appear, and when he reached there, his heart failed him and he was afraid to fight an inferior force, and then there was discovered "a want of ammunition to give battle."

No other brand of smoking tobacco is so celebrated, or has so extended a sale as "Lone Jack." In the United States its use is co-extensive with the country. Through wholesale agents located in the principal cities of fourteen different States, it is distributed to the trade and placed within the reach of consumers. It is exported to Europe, Asia, Africa and South America, and it is said that a package of "Lone Jack" can be bought in any town of importance in every part of the world. The founder and manufacturer of this superior smoking tobacco, is John W. Carroll, one of Lynchburg's most respected and public spirited citizens. He started life on the lowest rung of the ladder, and it was only by dint of constant and unceasing plodding and perseverance, backed by skill and principle, that he reached the top, where he now stands at the head of an immense business. Mr. Carroll was born in Staunton, Augusta County, Virginia, in 1832. Very early in life he suffered the loss of both parents and was obliged to make his own way in the world.

At the age of 14 he came to Lynchburg and entered as an apprentice in the shop of a cabinet maker; after a few years he abandoned this work and engaged in business with William Crumpton, a successful tobacconist of that day, whose daughter he afterwards married. For many years he labored faithfully and acquired a thorough knowledge of the tobacco business and laid the foundation for his subsequent remarkable success.

The name "Lone Jack" is a very peculiar one, and the way in which it came to be adopted reveals a strange and romantic incident which happened to Mr. Carroll, and which we here relate. About two years after Mr. Carroll had first established himself in the tobacco business (about the year 1850) when his fortunes were at a rather low ebb, and success in his chosen occupation seemed to him extremely doubtful, it chanced that, on a certain evening he sat down with a friend to play a game of "seven up." Each staked a dollar on every game, and through a long series of games Carroll was a constant loser; fortune seemed to have entirely deserted him. It was at a late hour, and with a feeling of extreme chagrin and disappointment, that he pulled out his last dollar and put it on the table. The critical moment arrived when his adversary stood six to his three and had the deal. Diamonds were trumps—and Carroll held one—a lone Jack: he looked at it almost with desperation. What chance had he to win the game? If his opponent held a single trump he was beaten. He hesitated, he quivered, but finally he gallantly stood his hand. As fortune would have it, the venture was successful; on that "Lone Jack" he scored high, low, Jack and the game, and won the stakes.

This lucky event made such an impression on his mind that he determined there and then to christen his leading brand of tobacco by the name, "Lone Jack." From such an accidental circumstance as the "turn of a card," did this notable brand of tobacco originate, which has since become known and celebrated in every clime, and brought both fame and fortune to its owner. When the civil war broke out Mr. Carroll promptly offered his services to his State, and during the long struggle and until its close, faithfully performed his duty as a soldier.

After peace was established he turned again to his business with redoubled energy, and it is since the war that his greatest triumphs have been gained. The quality and grade of smoking tobacco known as "Lone Jack" have always been the highest. The name is a synonyme of purity and excellence. The brand has never deteriorated, and as long as Mr. Carroll lives, it never will. "Lone Jack" is a tobacco entirely free from any mixture, adulteration, or flavoring whatever—the pure granulated leaf of the best and sweetest tobacco grown, free from stems, and uniform throughout in color, fineness, strength and flavor—affording to all true lovers of the weed a delicious, satisfying and enjoyable smoke. His buyers are stationed in all markets where the kind of leaf he requires is sold; when a really choice lot comes in, it is quickly snapped up and sent to the "Lone Jack" Factory. All the leaf used in the manufacture of "Lone Jack" is kept in stock two years before it is manufactured for consumption, a supply approximating a quarter of a million pounds being constantly on hand. It

is most carefully sorted, cured and manipulated, every process being subjected to the experienced and rigid inspection of the proprietor.

To maintain the high standard of excellence which his leading brand has always enjoyed, is Mr. Carroll's pride and joy. Although his financial success is almost unparalleled, he still sticks to his business with close application, and by reason of his unaffected manners and genial humor is exceedingly popular with everybody.

The old frame building first used by Mr. Carroll as a factory—"The Birthplace of Lone Jack"—as it is known, is still preserved by its owner as a memento of his less prosperous days, and in another part of this work a picture of it will be found. (See page 67.)

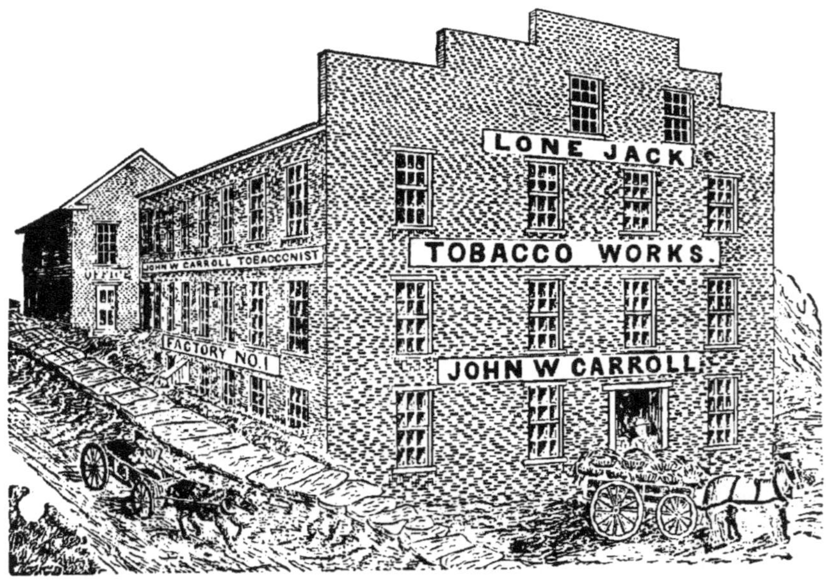

The present handsome and spacious factory is a large brick structure, located at 509 Grace Street, wherein all the operations of his extensive manufacturing business are carried on. The other kinds and qualities of smoking tobacco put up and sold by Mr. Carroll are "Brown Dick," "Game Cock" and "Grand Mogul." Although these brands are of a lower grade and sell at a much less price than "Lone Jack," still their reputation is well established, and their real merit is well understood.

An exceptional and super-excellent brand of smoking tobacco, known as "Fah-Kee," is put up by Mr. Carroll to supply a limited demand. As it sells for more than double the price of "Lone Jack," comparatively few people know anything about it. This quality was first ordered several years ago by a gentleman who supplied the foreign residents on the China Coast, and the brand was exclusively sold in that trade, but of late years, owing to the death of the gentleman who originated the brand, the restriction governing its sale has been withdrawn, and it is now sold to some extent in all parts of the country—mostly to people of wealth and connoisseurs of the weed.

Mr. Carroll's brands are all protected by patent, and he feels justified in warranting that tobaccos of his manufacture will remain sound, pure and aromatic in all latitudes and climates.

Mr. Carroll has occupied many positions of honor and trust in the community where he resides. He is now and for twenty-six years has been a member of the City Council (the last sixteen years its President) and for several years filled the office of President of the Lynchburg National Bank.

He is a gentleman of strict integrity and marked business ability; an energetic, unostentatious and painstaking man in both public and private affairs, who possesses the confidence and esteem of all classes of people.

COMMERCIAL AND GENERAL.

THE CHAMBER OF COMMERCE OF THE CITY OF LYNCHBURG.

The organization of this important and influential body resulted from a long felt necessity for "that concert of action and unity of purpose amongst the business men of the City" which was regarded as "essential to the full development of its material welfare and commercial prosperity." A meeting was called at the Lynch House on November 2nd, 1882, at which the general advantages of such an organization were unanimously conceded, and a committee appointed to report a Constitution and Rules of Order for the Association. Accordingly, at an adjourned meeting, held on the 2nd of December following, the Chamber of Commerce of the City of Lynchburg was formally organized, its general objects being proclaimed as follows:

> "The promotion of every scheme for the advancement of the commercial, manufacturing and monetary interests of this community, and the abatement of every grievance injuriously affecting such interests.
>
> "The establishment and application of uniform and equitable rules and usages of trade.
>
> "The collection and preservation of statistical information concerning the commerce, capital, production and growth of this city.
>
> "The speedy and economical settlement of differences amongst its members, without resort to litigation.
>
> "And the discussion of all questions affecting the interest of the capital, trade or manufactures of the city, and the pecuniary welfare of its citizens."

Since the date of its formation, the Chamber has been in active and useful operation, and has been the means of achieving much good to the industrial and mercantile interests of the City. The membership of the Chamber is numerous, and comprises the leading business men and firms among the Manufacturers, Bankers, Brokers, Merchants and Wholesale Dealers of Lynchburg. The first President of the Chamber was Mr. George M. Jones; the next was Capt.

Charles M. Blackford, who was succeeded by the present presiding officer.

The following gentlemen now compose the governing body of the Chamber, and their names cannot fail to inspire the utmost confidence among those who maintain commercial relations with the City: *President*, Jacob H. Franklin; *First Vice-President*, William H. Wren; *Second Vice-President*, William Kinnier; *Secretary*, Carter Glass; *Treasurer*, P. A. Krise; *Executive Committee*, C. H. Almond, C. M. Blackford, J. P. Bell, F. C. Brown, Joseph Cohn, J. R. Gilliam, Max Guggenheimer, Jr., Wm. A. Heffernan, Wm. Hurt, James W. Watts, Wm. A. Miller, Wm. A. Strother, C. W. Scott, George P. Watkins, J. Gordon Payne.

The annual meeting of the Chamber is held on the Second Tuesday in January. Quarterly meetings are also held on the Second Tuesdays in April, July and October, in each year, and regular meetings of the Executive Committee are held on the first Saturday of every month. Special meetings may be called at any time by the President, or acting President, or by any three members of the Executive Committee, due notice having been given to all the members.

THE LYNCHBURG TOBACCO ASSOCIATION

Until within the past few years, during which industrial interests of various kinds have been successfully undertaken in Lynchburg and its immediate vicinity, the commercial life of the City may be said to have been almost wholly dependent upon the Tobacco trade, in its numerous and always multiplying branches. Indeed this particular industry still holds by far the most important and conspicuous place among the varied pursuits which give employment to the capital, brains and muscle of the "Tobacco City's" inhabitants, and it is therefore very necessary that it should be fostered and encouraged with the utmost solicitude, and carefully fortified against all adverse possibilities from within or without. With these objects in view, and for the purpose of regulating the warehouse sales and exercising such supervisory authority over all transactions in Tobacco as would secure perfectly fair play between buyer and seller, broker and commission merchant, planter and manufacturer, this useful Association was organized in 1867. It is well-nigh impossible now to over-estimate the advantages which have accrued to the commercial interests of Lynchburg through the labors of this influential organization, whose list of membership bears the names of every tobacco manufacturer, warehouseman, broker and dealer in the City. The following gentlemen are the present Officers and Committeemen: *President*, John T. Edwards; *Vice-President*, R. H. T. Adams; *Secretary and Treasurer*, James Franklin, Jr.; *Supervisor of Weights*, S. W. Younger; *Executive Committee*, N. R. Bowman, (Chairman), R. L. Miller, C. L. Wright, S. W. Younger, James M. Booker, Jr., E. M. Heard, Wm. King, Jr., E. A. Allen, David Walker; *Arbitration Committee*, T. E. Murrell, (Chairman), J. H. Smith, H. H. Withers, John H. Flood, W. J. Collins.

The annual meeting of the Association is held on the first Monday

RESIDENCE OF MR. JOHN D. HOLT.
(CORNER OF WASHINGTON AND HARRISON STREETS.)

in October, and the regular monthly meetings on the first Monday of each month. Special meetings are called from time to time by the presiding officer or members of the Executive Committee as matters of urgency arise.

The Lynchburg Tobacco Association is perhaps the best organized and most systematic commercial body in Virginia, if not in the whole South; and it is but just to state that this state of efficiency has been attained, to a great extent, through the untiring energy and incessant vigilance of its President, Mr. John T. Edwards, who was elected to this position in October, 1885, and re-elected in 1886, after having previously served the Association as Vice-President. His membership dates back to 1873, since which time he has attended every meeting of the Association, except two; and on one of these occasions he was absent from the City. It is easy to believe that, with such an excellent example from the Chair, punctuality and other business-like properties are regarded as cardinal virtues by the members generally.

TRANSPORTATION.

Lynchburg lies at the intersection of three railroads which branch out in six different directions, namely: the Virginia Midland, northward to Washington and southward to North Carolina; the Norfolk & Western, southeastward to Norfolk and soutwestward to Tennessee, Georgia, &c.; and the Richmond & Alleghany, northeastward to Richmond and westward to the great coal fields of West Virginia.

THE VIRGINIA MIDLAND RAILWAY.

This line extends from the City of Washington, D. C., to Danville, on the border of North Carolina, passing through the productive Piedmont section of the State and entering the heart of the tobacco-growing region. It has branches from Manassas to Strasburg, in the Valley of Virginia, where it unites with the Baltimore & Ohio system; to Warrenton, in Fauquier County, to tap the rich grazing farms of that beautiful district; and to Rocky Mount, in Franklin County, to secure the tobacco and other valuable trade of the counties lying under the Blue Ridge in South Virginia.

At Washington and Alexandria the road makes close passenger and freight connection with the Baltimore & Ohio and the Pennsylvania Central systems; at Orange with a narrow gauge road to Fredericksburg. At Charlottesville it crosses and connects with the Chesapeake & Ohio Railroad, leading eastward to Richmond and deep water at Newport News, and westward to the coal and iron fields of West Virginia and to the Ohio River. At Lynchburg it intersects the Norfolk & Western and the Richmond & Alleghany Railroads. At Danville it unites with the Richmond & Danville Road, and, under the same general management, consolidates with what is known as the "Richmond & Danville System," which owns and controls nearly three thousand miles of railway, extending like a net-work through the Cotton States of the South.

THE NORFOLK & WESTERN RAILROAD.

With its eastern terminus at the magnificent port of Norfolk and Portsmouth, this road extends to Bristol, on the boundary line between Virginia and Tennessee, a distance of four hundred and eight miles, Lynchburg being exactly midway between these terminal points. Branches extend to City Point, at the confluence of the Appomattox and James Rivers; to the coal fields and iron mines of Pocahontas, in Tazewell County; to the great salt and plaster deposits at Saltville; and to the enormous coal and iron beds on Cripple Creek, in Wythe County.

This road connects at Petersburg with the lines running northward through Richmond and southward through Weldon, North Carolina; at Burkeville, with the Richmond & Danville system; at Lynchburg, with the Virginia Midland and the Richmond & Alleghany Roads; at Roanoke, with the Shenandoah Valley Railroad, forming another route southward; at Salem, with a branch of the Baltimore & Ohio; and at Bristol, with the East Tennessee, Virginia & Georgia Road and the great system which, through the medium of the Memphis and Charleston route, branches over the cotton region.

THE RICHMOND & ALLEGHANY RAILROAD.

This runs, as a completed road, along the bank of the James River from Richmond to Williamson's, a point on the Chesapeake & Ohio Railroad in Alleghany County, with a branch up the North River to Lexington, Virginia. It enters the heart of Richmond, and has access to the harbor and to all the other Railroads centring in that important city. It passes up the James River, through its fertile bottom lands, with switches to take granite at the quarries of Henrico and Fluvanna Counties, slate in Buckingham and Amherst, iron from several furnaces and ore from many mines.

At Lynchburg it unites with the Norfolk & Western and the Virginia Midland Railways. At Buchanan, it connects with the Shenandoah Valley Road; at Lexington, with the Baltimore & Ohio system, forming another route to the North and West; and at Williamson's it connects with the Chesapeake & Ohio, and thus reaches the Ohio River and the coal and iron of West Virginia.

It will thus be seen that LYNCHBURG is, perhaps, the best distributing point in the whole South. Not only has it six distinct lines of railway, radiating, as above shown, to all quarters, but there are competing routes in every direction.

Northward there are four: (1) By the Virginia Midland, all rail, through Washington and Baltimore. (2) By the Norfolk & Western, and steamers from Norfolk to Washington, Baltimore, Philadelphia, New York, Providence and Boston. (3) By the Richmond & Alleghany to Richmond and by steamers to northern ports. (4) By the Richmond & Alleghany and the Baltimore & Ohio, via Lexington.

Eastward there are three: (1) To Norfolk by the Norfolk & Western, and to Richmond by the same route, connecting at Burkeville with the Richmond & Danville Road. (2) To Richmond by the Richmond & Alleghany direct. (3) To Richmond by the Virginia Midland and the Chesapeake & Ohio at Charlottesville.

Southward there are two: (1) By the Virginia Midland and the Richmond & Danville system. (2) By the Norfolk & Western, the East Tennessee, Virginia & Georgia and the Memphis & Charleston lines.

Westward there are three: (1) By the Richmond & Alleghany and the Chesapeake & Ohio, and by the Richmond & Alleghany and the Baltimore & Ohio at Lexington. (2) By the Norfolk & Western. (3) By the Virginia Midland and the Chesapeake & Ohio, and by the Virginia Midland and the Baltimore & Ohio, at Strasburg.

These various lines are all strong and vigorous, and are all very actively competing for freight and passengers, thus securing Lynchburg, to a large extent, from the disastrous effects of transportation monopolies.

Other railroads are projected and chartered, which will, when completed, add considerably to the bulk of trade seeking this market. Chief among these is the

LYNCHBURG, HALIFAX & NORTH CAROLINA RAILROAD,

to the capital stock of which the City last year voted an appropriation of $250,000, and which may be regarded as a strictly local enterprise. The principal offices and the terminus of the Road will be in this City, and there is every reason to believe that the work of building the line will be commenced at once and prosecuted vigorously until completed to Durham, N. C., where it will connect with the Durham & Roxborough Railroad, thus bringing within our reach the fertile bottom lands of the Roanoke River, as well as the fine

THE FIRST BAPTIST CHURCH.
(CORNER OF COURT AND ELEVENTH STREETS.)

tobacco plantations of Halifax County. The recently elected officers of the Road are: *President*, Peter J. Otey; *Vice-President*, Wood Bouldin, Jr.; *Secretary*, Alexander McDonald; *Directors*, Mosby H. Payne, Jacob H. Franklin, J. R. Clark, Adam W. Nowlin, J. R. Lawson, John W. Clay, Robert W. Withers, H. A. Edmondson, Joseph Stebbins and Robert W. Watkins.

New lines of railway, and extensions of existing ones, are multiplying on all sides with astonishing rapidity, and especially is this the case with the roads which intersect at this point, and their immediate connections. The vast mineral wealth lying to the westward of us, and which has of late years attracted so much attention, is, of course, responsible, to a great extent, for this activity in railroad construction, which will probably continue until all the rich deposits of the neighboring sections have been brought within reach of their legitimate markets.

TOBACCO.

Situated centrally with relation to the great tobacco-growing region of Virginia, and enjoying exceptionally favorable transportation facilities, which bring all the great markets and seaports of the United States within easy and direct access, Lynchburg has always taken the lead not only as a mart and distributing point for the raw material, but also as a producer of the manufactured article, of all kinds and qualities, and has well earned the *sobriquet* by which she is widely known—"The Tobacco City." Ever since her foundation, the Town has been the depot for the tobacco grown within the district naturally tributary to her—from the days when the hogsheads were rolled along the public highways to market, down to the time when the introduction of railroads offered the planters a less expensive and far more expeditious method of transmitting their produce—and, as the "Devil's Weed," so named by the royal lunatic "Guid King Jamie," has always been the principal and most valuable crop cultivated in the surrounding counties, it has naturally exercised a ruling influence upon the commercial history of Lynchburg.

The average crop grown annually in this tributary section is about 75,000,000 pounds, and of this enormous aggregate at least two-thirds is handled by the warehousemen, dealers and manufacturers of this market. The handling of this immense quantity of leaf, and its manufacture into plug, twist and smoking tobacco, under almost innumerable brands, gives occupation, directly or indirectly, to the greater portion of Lynchburg's inhabitants. As the population increases and industries become more diversified, the influence of the Tobacco trade upon the aggregate business of the City will naturally diminish in proportion, but it is clear that for many years to come it will continue to hold the leading place among local industries, and that all others will remain to some extent dependent for their success upon its prosperity.

A great portion of the tobacco brought to this market still comes by wagons, direct from the neighboring plantations, but that grown in more remote districts also comes in considerable quantities over the lines of the several railroads centring here, and this latter class is increasing very rapidly. One reason for this increase is, that in many of the smaller towns and villages along the railroads that penetrate the tobacco-producing counties, warehouses and re-prizing "factories" have been established, and much of the crop so collected is forwarded in hogsheads to Lynchburg—which holds a sort of metropolitan relationship to the whole section—to be re-sold.

Six commodious warehouses supply the necessary accommodation for this large trade—one of which has been recently erected, in order to keep pace with the ever-growing bulk of arrivals. At all of these warehouses the leaf is sold "loose." In other markets it is sold in the hogshead, by sample, but it has been found more satisfactory here to offer it open on the warehouse floor, so that buyers may inspect every leaf, if they so desire, before making their purchases, and thus avoid all risks of dispute and controversy. A "Storage Warehouse" has also been opened lately, principally for the Western hogshead trade, which promises to become a great success.

The following table, taken from the official records of the Lynchburg Tobacco Association, show the actual sales of Leaf Tobacco on the warehouse floors for the last sixteen years—each year ending on October 1st—and it must be admitted that the figures bear testimony to a most gratifying increase :

1871.	17,425,530 lbs.	1876.	25,091,621 lbs.
1872.	14,323,708 "	1877.	19,699,775 "
1873.	20,214,748 "	1878.	28,318,183 "
1874.	18,206,321 "	1879.	21,143,217 "
1875.	14,127,430 "	1880.	25,062,881 "

1881. 20,090,822 lbs.	1884. 21,190,644 lbs.
1882. 20,127,208 "	1885. 29,495,758 "
1883. 24,620,811 "	1886. 37,462,979 "

In order that Lynchburg's position as a tobacco market may be clearly understood by the reader, the following extracts from the annual report presented to the Lynchburg Tobacco Association by its President, Mr. John T. Edwards, at the last annual meeting, are given :

* * * * * * * *

"The figures I shall give you to-day again place you at the head of the loose tobacco markets of the world, and there is no reason why you may not very soon be the peer of any market in the State for the sale of prized tobacco. One of Virginia's most gifted sons said : 'I know of no way of judging of the future but by the past ;' and, judging by the past, I ask you to contemplate what the near future of the tobacco trade of this beautiful and progressive City is to be. I do not propose to deal in imagination, or fancy pictures, but in stern reality, and figures that do not deceive.

"Look, if you please, at the following comparative statements and figures, and tell me if any market can truly show such increase in trade and substantial growth.

	Pounds.
"The average annual sales for fifteen years, per warehouses, from 1870 to 1884, inclusive, amounted to	20,657,162
Amount of tobacco sold in 1885 through warehouses	29,495,758
Increase percentage for 1885 over average sales for fifteen years preceding, 47 per cent.	
Total sales for 1885	38,306,939
Increase percentage, 90 per cent.	
Sales per warehouses for 1886	37,462,979
Sales per warehouses for 1885	29,495,758
Increase percentage in 1886 over sales of 1885, 27½ per cent.	
Sales not reported in 1886, per warehouses	8,708,799
Like sales in 1885	6,444,100
Increase percentage in 1886, 35 per cent.	
Resales in 1886, not included in above sales	3,160,272
Resales in 1885 as above	2,367,072
Increase percentage in 1886, less than 5 per cent.	
TOTAL SALES FOR THE YEAR 1886	49,332,050
Total sales for the year 1885	38,306,939
Increase percentage in 1886 over 1885, 29 per cent.	
INCREASE IN 1886 OVER AVERAGE SALES FOR FIFTEEN YEARS, FROM 1870 TO 1884, INCLUSIVE, 145 PER CENT.	
Amount of tobacco exported in 1886	21,710,723
Amount of tobacco exported in 1885	9,604,246
INCREASE PERCENTAGE EXPORTED IN 1886, 133 PER CENT.	

"The remainder of the purchases for 1886, amounting to 27,621,-

327 pounds, have been manufactured in Lynchburg, bought on domestic accounts and shipped to home markets. I am unable, as you are aware, from our system of selling tobacco, to ascertain the average price paid for tobacco sold here, but I assert it without fear of successful contradiction, that if it were possible to divide the dark and bright classes, the average on the former would far exceed that of any loose market of the State, and the largest proportion of the bright, being of the finest quality of cutters and wrappers, would far exceed any average on the bright markets of North Carolina and this State.

* * * * * * * *

"In my last address I called your attention to the importance of

CONFEDERATE SOLDIERS' MONUMENT.
(IN THE METHODIST CEMETERY.)

constructing the Lynchburg, Halifax and Durham Railroad. You have acted wisely, and now this Railroad is about to be constructed through the finest tobacco counties of Virginia and North Carolina. With the completion of this Railroad, I predict an increase in your trade annually of 5,000,000 to 10,000,000 pounds tobacco, to say nothing of other benefits to be derived from it, both by the farmers along the line and the citizens of Lynchburg. South Boston, that flourishing and enterprising town of Halifax, is soon to be closely allied with you. Geographically, you occupy a position superior to any in the State, as a distributing market. You have railroads stretching out in every direction, and connection with every tobacco market of the world. Your loose tobacco market is now favorably known to every nation and every city of the world. Your export trade is rapidly increasing. Your export buyers are strong competitors on all classes of tobacco. You have orders for all the finest wrappers, finest canary cutters, finest smokers, finest dark shipping, for which your market is celebrated, as well as all the lower classes.

* * * * * * * *

"Nothwithstanding the large increase in your receipts this year through the warehouses, it will be seen at a glance that the demands of the trade have not been satisfied. Let the producers look to this and send their tobacco direct to the market that shows a demand for it."

As a Leaf Tobacco market Lynchburg, therefore, heads the list. As a Tobacco manufacturing point she stands fifth. In addition to the railroads now centring here, the Lynchburg, Halifax & Durham road, penetrating some of the richest tobacco-growing counties in Virginia and North Carolina, will shortly be opened, thus forming another important feeder to the trade of the City.

With all these advantages, it must be evident that Lynchburg's future, as a great central depot for the staple product of this region—to say nothing of her other industries and general commerce—is fully assured.

There are in the City to-day twenty-five houses engaged in the manufacture of Chewing Tobacco—plug and twist—and nine in the manufacture of Smoking Tobacco—including the celebrated and incomparable "Lone Jack"; three Cigarette Factories; Six Tobacco Warehouses; one Tobacco Storage Warehouse; thirty-three Tobacco Leaf Dealers, who buy immense quantities of tobacco, as agents and on orders, for domestic and foreign markets; nine Tobacco Commission Merchants; one manufacturer of snuff; one of Tobacco Extract and one Fertilizer Factory—the only one in the world—the base of whose excellent product is Tobacco. Incidentally to the trade there are manufacturers of Tobacco Boxes, Hogsheads, Specific Machinery, &c., while the number of citizens, of all classes, immediately dependent on this branch of trade for their livelihood, would aggregate several thousands.

STATISTICAL REVIEW—1868 TO 1883.

The latest "Annual Report" of the Lynchburg Chamber of Commerce, which contains statistical information of any special value, was issued in 1884, and the subjoined extracts are selected from the address of its then President, Capt. Charles M. Blackford, delivered on the 8th of January in that year:

"When the war closed, Lynchburg, like all other Southern cities, was completely prostrate. Its enormous slave property was valueless; all its banks and monetary institutions were hopelessly insolvent; its currency by one blow reduced to worthless paper; personal property was all gone, and real estate reduced to a minimum in value; every industry destroyed; labor disorganized; government unstable, and the future so uncertain that men's hearts failed them for fear. Yet amidst darkness and gloom, with patient toil and frugal life, our people went to work, and to work with a vim, and in three years had accomplished wonders, and had gotten themselves into line and the machinery of business fairly going.

"Now, giving our people these three years to get into position, let us see what has been done since.

"Full statistics of trade and progress have not been preserved. Still, there are some facts undisputed, by a comparison of which you can measure the result of your labors.

"For example: while the exact figures cannot be given, it is considerably understating them to say that from 1868 to 1883 the population has more than doubled.

"In 1868 the total real and personal property of Lynchburg assessed for taxation, amounted to $3,264,705; in 1883 to $9,797,921, or three times as much, and this does not include the capital in business, which comes under the head of license tax.

"From the data which have been gathered by our agent, I am safe in making the following, as an approximate estimate of the values owned in Lynchburg in 1883:

Amount of real estate	$5,406,641
Personal property, as taxed	3,891,271
Engaged in trade, as capital and otherwise	2,897,962
U. S. Bonds and other personal property, not listed, estimated	500,000
Total property of the city	$12,695,874

"This shows that, while the population was doubled in this period, the wealth is four times as great.

"This estimate of population and property is made with due regard to the extension of the City limits, which was made between the two dates compared. In ascertaining the population in 1868, I take the figures of a local census which included all the territory subsequently incorporated into the City, and the values are taken from the values assessed for taxation under the railroad tax, which extended for half a mile around the former limits, and included all the territory taken in by the extension of the limits.

"Another interesting comparison is found in the statements of the banking institutions of the City.

"The true banking capital of a place is not the mere par of the aggregate capital stock of the different banks. It is the money which, through the instrumentality of the banks, is centralized in a place, and is available to the merchant or manufacturer who desires to borrow. This, of course, includes under the head of 'Banking Capital,' the aggregate capital, surplus and deposits of all the banks; for this aggregate, after deducting what is invested in real estate, office furniture and other like property, and what cash is necessarily kept on hand, is what the banks have to lend out and thus put into the channels of trade.

"In the beginning of 1868, the aggregate capital, surplus and deposits of all the banks of Lynchburg amounted only to $537,811.82, of which, so high was the rate of discount, [then twelve per centum] that only $276,359.45 was lent out and represented by bills receivable.

"In 1883, the aggregate capital, surplus and deposits, amounts to $3,428,078.17—over six times as much—and the loans, instead of being $276,359.45, as in 1868, aggregate an average of *two and one-half millions*—nearly ten times as much, but are at a rate of discount of only six per centum.

"Nor is this great increase the only remarkable disclosure made by this inspection of the bank statements. The bills receivable of the banks and bankers of the city averaged for 1883, an aggregate of about $2,500,000. The average duration of the negotiable paper discounted by banks is ninety days, and hence the whole $2,500,000 was renewed, some of it in the same, but the most of it in different hands, four times during the year; and therefore the total discounts of the banks of Lynchburg for the year 1883 aggregated *ten millions of dollars*, and I speak advisedly, as the President of a bank in full accord with the other banks, and by their authority, when I announce that out of this large sum so lent out in this community during the past year, *not one cent was lost or suspended*. The same thing, I believe, can not be said by any other place of the same size and doing the same amount of business in the United States.

"The statistics from the railroads have not all been furnished yet; but enough is before me to justify a statement that the tonnage to and from Lynchburg during the past year was about nine time as much as it was ten years ago.

* * * * * * *

"During the past ten years, the trade and manufacture of tobacco has increased, but not in proportion with the advance of other industries, a fact which is significant, and for which many reasons are given.

"In 1873, 18,206,321 pounds of leaf tobacco were sold in Lynchburg; in 1883, 24,620,811 pounds. In 1873, 4,503,337 pounds of tobacco were manufactured here; in 1883, 6,061,568 pounds.

"Why this trade alone has lagged in the race, is a very difficult question to answer.

* * * * * * * *

"For one I have no great apprehension that the tobacco trade of this City will decline. There is too much energy and capital in it for that, but the fact is the place has outgrown this particular traffic. Thirty years ago, aye, twenty years ago, when Lynchburg won and deserved the title of 'The Tobacco City,' when capital and industry

RESIDENCES ON CHURCH STREET.
MR. CHARLES W. BUTTON. DR. D. A. LANGHORNE.

sought no other channel, when a citizen was a tobacconist or nothing, and when a stranger, to use the language of the sable poet, was only

'Gwine down to Lynchburg town,
To carry his tobacco down dar.'

this place was dependent on that trade exclusively. This is not now the case, not because of any decline in the tobacco trade, but because other enterprises have to so much larger extent occupied the industries of our people, and have made such rapid growth that tobacco, while it is still indisputably king, and will be so for many years to come, finds a rival not to be despised, and all good citizens must rejoice that such is the case.

"Long since the war the commercial vigor of Lynchburg was confined to the retail trade. Now the retail trade has greatly increased in bulk and in profit, and in addition, house after house is being started, devoted exclusively to the wholesale business in distinct articles.

"The merchant can here be supplied now with groceries, dry goods, hard-ware, boots and shoes, hats and caps, drugs and medicines, all from different houses, and at prices so low that those who buy once are sure to come again. Nor do these merchants sit quietly in their counting rooms and wait for trade to come to them, as in the Arcadian days of John Hollins, John G. Meem and Henry Davis.

"Every train that leaves, carries a commercial traveller on his missionary tour in behalf of his employer in particular, and Lynchburg in general, and I am told that whenever two or three are gathered together within a radius of hundreds of miles, there will be found a Lynchburg drummer in the midst, plying his vocation with such zeal that the more fastidious representatives of the larger cities retire in disgust from the ground, knowing that if it is thus in the green tree, competition will be a farce in the dry.

"If one will start from the abutment of the beautiful dam which has just been finished across the river, and which will greatly increase our water power, and pass down to the end of this level on the canal, the evidence of recent growth and development is very apparent"—(Here are enumerated Flour Mills, Foundries and Machine Shops, Gas Works, Lumber Yards, the new City Pump House, Planing Mills, Sash, Blind and Door Factories, Furnaces, Furniture Factory, Sumac Mill, Bark and Dye Works, Barytes Mill and "the long line of freight trains, bulked from three roads, and with cars whose labels trace their homes South as far as Texas, West to the Rocky Mountains and North to the Grand Trunk")—"all tell of new enterprise, of diverted capital, and of successful endeavors, and tell a tale to which others are listening with anxious ear.

* * * * * * * *

"I have thus grouped some of these new enterprises that we may see the City is making its departure into other channels than tobacco. But much, much more can and must be done. How much room have we for cotton and woolen factories, for manufactories of agricultural implements, of carriages and wagons, of paper, wooden ware, spokes, staves, fertilizers, leather, boots and shoes, hats and caps, drugs and medicines, stoves and castings of like nature, furniture, pottery, glass and all the infinite variety of iron ware; indeed all the numberless articles which man's luxuries or necessities demand.

"We have room in abundance, and there is still vast unused water power on this and the level above the City, or, if steam is preferred as a motive power, coal is now reduced to a figure which makes it available, and by circling the town with a railway, switching off from the

Midland track, near Karn & Hickson's brick yard, and running toward the Dirt Bridge or Fair Grounds, and possibly connecting with the Norfolk & Western road, very ample accommodations can be provided for any new enterprise at very moderate cost.

"Situated as this City is, in the midst of a cheap and healthy country, where labor and money are cheap; where power, either by water or steam can be economically applied; where the raw material is daily passing by us to seek distant factories; where the climate is so moderate that cyclones and tornadoes are unknown, and where the zero point is almost unnoted on the thermometer, and men can do out-door work eleven and a half out of the twelve months of the

PROPERTY OF THE LYNCHBURG AGRICULTURAL AND MECHANICAL SOCIETY.
(THE MAIN BUILDING AND GRAND STANDS FROM THE RACE TRACK.)

year, and where six railways ray out in six different directions, and connect with the whole network of the land, North, South, East and West—there is no place which so commends itself to the manufacturer as a distributing point for his wares, or where he can sit so close to the gateways of the great marts and enjoy their benefits and yet escape their burden of expense."

THE LYNCHBURG AGRICULTURAL AND MECHANICAL SOCIETY

was organized in May, 1869, and in October of the same year held its first annual Fair in the beautiful and extensive grounds belonging to the Society, near the southwestern boundary of the City. Col. George P. Tayloe, of Roanoke, was chosen as the first President, and the late Mr. T. C. S. Ferguson, of Lynchburg, Chairman of the Executive Committee, with Mr. Alexander McDonald Secretary and Treasurer. Under the able management of these excellent officers, assisted by an Executive Committee comprising some of the most substantial citizens of Lynchburg and the neighboring counties, the success of the organization was assured from its inception. Under the immediate supervision of Mr. Ferguson, with the benefit of his experience and jndgment, the Society expended about $20,000 during the first summer and autumn of its existence, in beautifying the grounds, erecting buildings—pavilions, stalls, &c.—and in laying out and grading the race track.

The Society has had some reverses and many difficulties to contend with, on account of unseasonable weather, floods, financial stringency and other causes, but it has always managed to hold its own, and more, not having failed once, since its organization, to give to this community and section of country the benefit of its Annual Exhibition; and during that period it has distributed to its friends and patrons, in the way of premiums and current expenses, about $150,000, besides having been the means of attracting hundreds of thousands of dollars in trade to the City, that might otherwise have gone elsewhere. The advantages that the Society has conferred upon Lynchburg are beyond any computation.

Col. Tayloe was succeeded as President by Mr. Joseph Cloyd, of Pulaski, and he, in turn, by Mr. George W. Palmer, of Smyth County. Major D. P. Graham, of Wythe, was the next President, succeeded by Mr. Charles M. Blackford, of this City. At the annual meeting held on May 2nd of this year, Senator John W. Daniel was unanimously elected the President of the Society for the current year, Mr. Blackford having declined re-election. Mr. Blackford was also the second chairman of the Executive Committee; Mr. B. H. Nowlin, third; and Mr. John W. Carroll, fourth. Mr. E. J. Folkes succeeded Mr. Carroll, and is, and has been for five years, a most efficient incumbent of this most responsible position. It is due to Mr. Folkes to say that the signal success of the Centennial Celebration, held last year (1886) was owing more to him than to any other individual, because of his indefatigable personal supervision and direction of the preparations, together with the great ability and excellent judgment he exercised in consummating the desired object.

Many eminent statesmen and orators have, from time to time, honored the Society with their presence, and addressed the gathered multitudes, on the occasion of the Annual Exhibitions at the Fair Grounds. The list would be too extended if all were enumerated, but it may not be amiss to mention Hon. A. G. Thurman, a native Lynchburger, Senator Vance, Hon. B. Johnson Barbour, Governor Gilbert C. Walker, Hon. Thomas S. Bocock, Hon. A. R. Boteler,

PROPERTY OF THE LYNCHBURG AGRICULTURAL AND MECHANICAL SOCIETY.
(VIEW OF THE FAIR GROUNDS FROM THE MAIN BUILDING.)

Hon. J. L. M. Curry, Judge Fullerton, of New York, General Fitzhugh Lee, the present Governor of Virginia, Rev. Dr. Fitzgerald, another native Lynchburger, Capt. James Barron Hope, of Norfolk, and Lynchburg's distinguished son and favorite orator, Senator John W. Daniel.

At the annual meeting of the Life Members of the Agricultural Society in 1884, a preamble and resolution were introduced by Mr. Alexander McDonald, and unanimously adopted, setting forth the fact that the year 1886 would be the Centennial of Lynchburg's existence, and suggesting, thus early, the propriety of having the Executive Committee take the initiative in celebrating it appropriately.

Acting upon this suggestion, co-operative committees from other organizations in the City were appointed, and, by the faithful, united and harmonious work of all, the great and memorable Celebration of last year was the result. To Mr. McDonald is due the credit of originating the idea of the Centennial and in arranging and carrying out the programme, and it is also his due to add that no one worked more laboriously to make it a success in every particular. The Trades Parade would have reflected credit upon a city of much greater pretensions than Lynchburg. It was the surprise and delight of all who saw it. Various were the attractions during the festival, and immense crowds thronged the streets, to the number of many thousands in excess of any previous concourse here. It was, in fact, a glorious reunion, and will be long remembered by all who took part in it. One of the many prominent features of the celebration was the planting of a "Centennial Oak" in the Fair Grounds, with impressive and interesting ceremonies.

The Lynchburg Agricultural and Mechanical Society is now in the full tide of prosperity, being entirely free from debt and having a surplus in its treasury. The Managers of its affairs point with just pride to its prosperous condition—the most prosperous by far of all similar organizations in the State. Whilst there are many who have contributed liberally of their time and money to bring about this state of affairs, all will agree that to the accomplished editor of the *Virginian*, Mr. Alexander McDonald, the community is indebted more than to any one else, because of his ever watchful and faithful care in the management of the Society's interests, in his dual capacity of Secretary and Treasurer. Those who have the best opportunity of knowing will bear willing testimony to the correctness of this statement; and further, that, except for Mr. McDonald's efforts, the Society would long since have languished and died. The fact of his having been re-elected unanimously every year to this responsible office, is ample evidence of the confidence and appreciation in which he is held by the members and managers of the Society.

The next Fair will be held in October of this year, and the Executive Committee are already making preparations, by improving the race track, grading, beautifying, building, planting, &c., and it is believed that this will be the most extensive and attractive exhibition ever given under the auspices of the Society.

The following are the present officers: *President*, John W. Daniel; *Chairman of Executive Committee*, E. J. Folkes; *Secretary and Treasurer*, Alexander McDonald; *Executive Committee*, E. J. Folkes, F. D. Johnson, E. A. Craighill, Ridgway Holt, R. L. Miller, George D. Witt, James R. Kyle, L. P. Shaner, W. D. Adams, Samuel Tyree, E. C. Hamner, S. W. Nowlin, G. W. Smith, W. O. Johnson and Joseph Cohn.

BANKS AND BANKERS.

It is beyond question that in the matter of sound and liberal financial institutions Lynchburg is extremely fortunate. These form the bulwarks of trade in all mercantile and industrial communities, and frequently offer the safest and most satisfactory investment for floating capital. There are five incorporated Banks in the City—four National and one State—besides two private Bankers. These represent resources which in the aggregate amount to several millions of dollars—a sum fully adequate to all the demands which the large trade of the City is likely to make upon it. No difficulty is experienced by the manufacturers, brokers and other business men in obtaining as much money as they require, at all times and at reasonable rates, on good commercial paper. In fact, the Banks are competitors for mercantile discounts, and are always ready and willing to aid the reputable merchant and manufacturer in the prosecution of his legitimate business. The Lynchburg Banks are well and prudently managed, and are all paying handsome dividends. In evidence of this it may be stated that they have been entirely unaffected by the "runs" and "panics" which have proved so disastrous to the banking establishments of other Virginia cities during the last few years.

HOTELS.

On arriving at Lynchburg for the first time, the stranger cannot fail to be impressed most favorably with the superiority of our Hotel accommodations; and this is admitted to be one of the best criterions by which to gauge the general commercial prosperity—or otherwise—of every city. It must be confessed that in this respect many of our Southern provincial towns are sadly deficient, and the traveller is certain to be agreeably surprised at the comfort and elegance with which he finds himself surrounded when he first accepts the hospitality of the "Hill City." Situated at the intersection of several busy railroads, Lynchburg receives and entertains many thousands of transient visitors during the year, and first-class hotels have been, for many years past, not only an absolute necessity to the public but also a source of handsome revenue to their proprietors, who vie with each other in supplying the wants and increasing the comforts of their guests.

Our Hotels are all that the most fastidious could desire—lofty, commodious, well lighted and well ventilated, within easy reach of railroad depots, churches, places of amusement, street railways, banks, stores, &c.; well furnished and provided with parlors and reception rooms; cleanly, comfortable, well managed and devoid of those trifling but numerous discomforts which usually render hotel life so unattractive. Their tables abound in all seasonable luxuries, and the large patronage which they enjoy is the best possible testimonial to their excellence.

IRON WORKS, FOUNDRIES, &c.

The proximity of Lynchburg to the great coal and iron fields of Western Virginia has naturally led to the establishment at this point of Furnaces and Iron Works, of which there are now three in extensive operation. All of these have recently enlarged their capital with a view to expanding their capacity and increasing their products. They are all busy and prosperous, with every prospect of continued success. Pig Iron of the finest quality is manufactured from the ores of this district, while the Nails, Bars, Spikes, &c., made here in large quantities are unsurpassed, and command a ready market as rapidly as they can be turned out. Castings for Agricultural Implements and Machinery of all kinds are also among the products of our local foundries. In addition to these there are established agencies of Harvesting Machines of various popular makes, and of those numerous other inventions which have become indispensable to the modern agriculturist and manufacturer. The means of supplying, renewing and repairing is thus brought within the reach of all who employ engines and other mechanical contrivances, either in tobacco factories, grist or saw mills, or in the simpler but not less essential operations of the farm.

DRUGS AND CHEMICALS.

The bulk of business done in these important commodities, in

Lynchburg, is much more considerable than would be supposed by the uninitiated, and is conducted by two wholesale and about a dozen retail houses, whose united sales reach the handsome sum of half a million dollars, or thereabouts, annually. The stocks kept by these establishments are large and varied, and several of our druggists have earned a wide and honorable reputation through the excellence of the goods they supply, as well as through the agency of certain "specialties" which they put up.

The wholesale and manufacturing representatives of this branch of trade have done valuable service to the City, for their enterprise has been the means of retaining and disbursing among our own people, in the form of wages, and otherwise, thousands of dollars which formerly went to Richmond, Baltimore, Philadelphia, and other markets, in payment for the same goods which can now be supplied at home, on equally favorable terms.

Besides Drugs and Chemicals, all our wholesale and some of our retail houses carry full lines of Paints and Oils, Perfumery, Spices, Seeds, Patent Medicines, Fancy and Toilet Articles, and numerous other commodities not strictly akin to pharmacy, such as Tobacco, Cigars, Cigarettes, &c. Our principal wholesale drug trade is carried on with Southwest Virginia, Tennessee, the two Carolinas and Georgia, while all the Southern and Middle States have been made more or less familiar with Lynchburg's enterprise in this line. Nor is this all. From New York, Boston, Philadelphia, Chicago, Denver, San Francisco, Austin, and all the principal cities of the Union, orders have been received for preparations compounded here, and it is a matter of record, most gratifying to the manufacturers, that these preparations have been enquired for and purchased in London and Paris, as well as in other European capitals. Even distant Australia has furnished an applicant for the agency of one of Lynchburg's proprietary medicines, and it is therefore quite reasonable to expect that the name and fame of our City will yet overspread the civilized world as the birth place and home of more than one commercial celebrity.

BOOKS, STATIONERY, &c.

The quality and quantity of reading matter in circulation among the people of any community will be found to be a very accurate test of their intellectual capacity and refinement. Where there are well patronized book stores, carrying large and well-selected assortments of standard literature, there will also most certainly be found a large proportion of cultivated and well-informed readers. And this may justly be claimed for Lynchburg, where the book business is conducted by men whose own high education and mental culture eminently qualify them to cater to the intellectual requirements of their neighbors. We have several handsome and well-stocked Book and Stationery Stores, where all commodities usually kept by first-class establishments of the kind are to be found in great abundance and endless variety, including choice paintings, engravings, photographs, and a host of other articles which may be grouped under the generic term "Fancy." In some cases the Book and Stationery business is combined with that of Pianos, Organs and Music, and our dealers represent the most famous factories in the country, and always keep on hand a large selection of first-class instruments.

GROCERS AND COMMISSION MERCHANTS.

These two important branches of Lynchburg's trade are here consolidated, for the reason that they are too closely allied to each other to admit of separate treatment. United, they cover a vast field and embrace many interests. Indeed, there is no department of commercial enterprise represented in the City which employs so much capital, engages so many of our leading business men, or exercises so wide-spread an influence over the whole territory which recognizes Lynchburg as its principal or central market. It is customary among our wholesale grocers to act also as commission merchants, and *vice versa*. Vast quantities of tobacco, grain, bacon, poultry and other kinds of produce, are received here for sale on commission, and the consignments are often accompanied by orders for provisions or cash. An open account is often kept by the planter with his Commission Merchant, who advances what goods, fertilizers and money may be required by his country customer, from harvest to harvest, and it occasionally happens that the latter is unable, through misfortune or some other cause, to make a settlement even at harvest time, in which event his Commission Merchant must "carry" him till the following year, taking a mortgage lien upon land or future crops, as security. It will be seen that considerable capital is required to carry on a business of this kind; and it may be here stated, without fear of contradiction, that in no town in the United States can be found a more sound, solvent and successful body of business men than the Grocers and Commission Merchants of Lynchburg, in proportion to the population and the amount of capital involved.

RESIDENCE OF MR. JOSEPH COHN.
(CHURCH STREET, NEAR SIXTH.)

FURNITURE.

This trade has assumed much importance in Lynchburg of late years, and now employs a large cash capital. Ordinary household necessaries could always be obtained here as well as elsewhere, but the handsomer and more expensive articles were generally sought at Richmond, or even still further away, until those now engaged in the business wisely took advantage of the opportunity thus offered to local enterprise. Our Furniture Warerooms now contain large and varied assortments of stock, and every taste and every pocket can be suited, at factory prices, whether the articles be required for parlor, dining room, chamber, office or school. There are several firms engaged here in this business, and they can afford to sell their goods at reasonable figures, as they make their purchases at the manufactories and obtain the most favorable terms. The out-lying districts of this and adjoining States find this a most advantageous market at which to make their purchases, and each year brings increased business to our dealers. Here, as in other places, there are those to be met with who refuse to acknowledge genuine excellence unless they import it direct from some distant market; but experience has taught the great majority of consumers that it is more economical, as well as infinitely more satisfactory, to deal with merchants whom they know personally and meet every day, reliable and responsible business men, who are always accessible when, through some accident or unexpected flaw, a guarantee may have to be made good.

WEARING APPAREL.

The above words are intended only to apply, in this instance, to Boots and Shoes, Hats and Caps, Clothiers' and Tailors' Goods, and Men's Furnishing Goods generally, and not to those unfathomable mysteries of feminine attire which are distracting even to think upon, and cannot possibly be either enumerated or described. These combined interests require considerable capital, and it is estimated that in Lynchburg not less than a quarter of a million of dollars is invested in them. The Boot and Shoe business, in which there is one large house doing an *exclusively* wholesale trade, is very far reaching, and goods supplied by Lynchburg houses may be found in every portion of Central and Western Virginia, in the two Carolinas, Georgia, Alabama, Tennessee and other Southern States. Hats and Caps, which also have an exclusively wholesale representative here, form another link in the chain which binds us commercially to the people of adjoining States, and sales in this line are heavy, especially in Virginia, North Carolina and Tennessee, where the bulk of the business is done. The same may be truly said of Clothiers' and Tailors' Goods and Men's Furnishing Goods, the trade in which is extending gradually, and will doubtless some day overspread a much more extended territory. All these different branches of Lynchburg's business are in the hands of sterling, practical men, who are intimately acquainted with the wants of their respective trades and thoroughly understand them in their most minute details. Having sufficient working capital, they are enabled to take advantage of every fluctuation of the market, and to buy up at low figures whatever may be suitable to their business. By these means they can often sell to the retail trade and individual consumers at better prices than the manufacturer would be willing to accept during his busy season.

DRY GOODS, NOTIONS, &c.

No attempt will be made here to depict the wonders or solve the mysteries of that "Woman's Paradise," a first-class Dry Goods Store, a mere catalogue of whose ordinary stock would fill many a close-writ page. Suffice it to say that Lynchburg can show as handsome and as well-stocked establishments devoted to this particular class of merchandise as any city in Virginia, or elsewhere in the Southern Land. She can also boast of at least one mammoth concern, whose trade is exclusively wholesale, and whose annual business it would require seven figures to compute. Until within the past few years the wholesale trade of Lynchburg, in this as in all other departments, was comparatively unimportant, but only for the reason that no persistent experiment in that direction had been made. The uniform success which has crowned those enterprising houses which have led the van in establishing the City as a great wholesale depot has already encouraged several others to follow their good example, and it is not overstating the case to assert that to-day the "Hill City" has few equals in the whole South as a trade centre. Our principal Dry Goods and Notions Stores are on Main Street and many of them carry heavy stocks of all those articles belonging to their trade, including full lines of carpets, of all descriptions and the product of all lands, as well as mats, rugs, druggets, and other similar wares. All their goods are guaranteed not to exceed Northern prices, and their assortments are as complete as are to be met with in any other city.

MISCELLANEOUS TRADES.

In the preceding pages, special attention has been directed, under distinctive headings, to several of the principal branches of trade and industry which engage the manufacturing and mercantile classes of Lynchburg, and it must be conceded that not only does the present condition of her affairs make a most creditable showing, but also that her existing advantages are in a fair way to be considerably augmented, and that her future is rich in promises of continually increasing prosperity—promises which will certainly be redeemed, provided her people remain faithful to themselves and to their traditions.

In addition to the more prominent subjects already reviewed, there are others, too numerous for separate classification, and yet too productive of good, in their combined influence upon the community, to justify their being passed by without mention. Among the industries which may be regarded as incidental to the enormous tobacco interests of the City, the manufacture of Hogsheads and Tobacco Boxes occupies a prominent position and gives employment to a large number of mechanics. The demand for these products by local tobacco shippers and manufacturers is naturally very considerable; but it is not confined to the City, orders being constantly received from neighboring towns along the several lines of railroad. A Broom and Brush factory has recently been established here, and its capacity is already taxed to fill orders for the local trade. This will prove of great advantage not only to those actually engaged in the business, but also as suggesting to the farmers of this district a new and profitable crop. The phenomenal success of our Fertilizer and Insecticide factory—the only one in the world the basis of whose product is tobacco—has been most gratifying to the whole community, as well as to its projectors and proprietors, the value of whose ingenious formula has been proved beyond controversy under the severest tests. The Printing and Binding establishments of the City defy successful competition as regards both the quality and the price of the work they turn out. Every visitor to the City is struck at once with the style and excellence of the carriages and horses—the property of our enterprising Livery Stable proprietors—which are always to be seen on our streets. There is perhaps no town in the South where better conveyances and saddle horses can be hired than in Lynchburg. This is due in great measure to the almost precipitous character of many of our thoroughfares, on which inferior horseflesh and defective vehicles would be worse than useless. In this connection it may be stated that there are several carriage, buggy, cart and wagon builders in the City who turn out first-class work and are highly esteemed throughout the neighboring districts. The City Cemeteries and rural Graveyards for many miles around are supplied with beautiful marble and granite shafts and tomb-stones which bear the "imprint" of a well known Lynchburg sculptor, as do also many of the ornaments which adorn our handsome churches and residences. The windows and show cases of our Jewelry Stores sparkle with rich gems and present a most attractive assortment of watches, clocks, gold and silver ware, and such other articles as pertain to this department of trade, which here embraces spectacles, eye-glasses and opticians' goods generally. Fine engraving on stone and metal, designing and repairing of all kinds, can be executed here in true artistic style, while orders for Lynchburg watches are received from even the most distant points in the United States with increasing frequency. In the matter of Hardware, Stoves, Tinware, Cutlery, and other kindred commodities, the business done here is simply enormous, and there is no need to pass Lynchburg in search of any article in this line, as the whole catalogue can be found in stock at any of our leading houses, of first-class quality, and at reasonable prices. The manufacture of Ice from distilled water is among the recent industrial experiments of the City, and, so far, the enterprise has been rewarded with complete success. This now indispensable article of daily consumption is furnished here at half-a-cent per pound, or, in larger quantities, at five dollars per ton. The Ice is absolutely pure, and, at the prices above quoted, is now within the reach of all classes of consumers. Other important industries are in full and successful operation in and around the City, to wit: Grist, Saw and Planing Mills, Door, Sash and Blind Factories, Bark Mills, Dye Works, Barytes Mills, Stone Quarries, and a score more, which, however, have not yet attained special prominence. A tour of the City will reveal to the observant visitor such an array of magnificent new structures—Churches, Public Buildings, Private Residences, Factories, Stores and Warehouses,—that any further eulogy of our Architects, Contractors and dealers in Builders' Materials would be regarded by him as entirely superfluous. This is a great mart for Horses and Mules, which are extensively dealt in by our Livery Stable proprietors. The best stock for any and all purposes can be obtained here at all times and at such prices as to suit all purchasers. The Lynchburg Agricultural and Mechanical Society has done much towards establishing this City as a great cattle and live stock market also, and our leading Butchers deal largely in live as well as dead meat of the finest quality. Such goods as China and Glass Ware are to be found here in as great variety and at as low prices as in the large Northern Cities. Our Painters, Plumbers, Tinners, Boot and Shoe Makers, Blacksmiths and mechanics of all kinds furnish excellent work, each in his own line; while our Photographic Artists turn out first-class work in all styles, and faithfully reproduce, in most becoming manner, the very superior efforts of those other artists, the Milliners and Tailors. Stencil cutting and stamp designing have also their efficient representatives here, as have also all classes of mechanical and artistic contrivances, sewing machines, electrical machinery, &c. Musical Instruments of every description can be purchased, renewed and repaired. Our Confectionery establishments are unrivalled in the variety, and excellence of their delicious wares. In short, for a city of its size and population, there cannot be found one anywhere in which the necessaries, comforts and luxuries of life, in all conceivable forms, are more abundant or more easily obtainable than they are in Lynchburg, and if those who have been accustomed to send to distant points for their supplies will only give our merchants, manufacturers and mechanics a fair trial, they will certainly have no cause to regret the experiment, which will no doubt result in securing their permanent patronage for our "home trade."

THE LOCAL PRESS.

THE LYNCHBURG VIRGINIAN.

This venerable and widely known journal, which has only one senior in the State, was established in 1808, when Lynchburg was a comparatively small and unimportant town. It was launched as "The Lynchburg Press," but when, in 1820, it came into the hands of the late John Hampden Pleasants—one of the most distinguished journalists the State of Virginia has ever produced—its name was changed to "The Lynchburg *Virginian,*" and has so remained ever since.

When Mr. Pleasants left the *Virginian* to take up his residence at the Capital, where he became the founder of the Richmond *Whig*, Richard H. Toler succeeded to the editorship of this paper, and, upon his transfer some years afterwards to the Richmond *Whig*, William M. Blackford became his successor here. Upon the retirement of Mr. Blackford, A. W. C. Terry assumed the duties of editor of the *Virginian*, and continued in their discharge until his death, which occurred in 1851. James McDonald was then installed in the editorial chair which he occupied till the beginning of 1857, when the paper was purchased by Charles W. Button, who became editor and continued in that position until July, 1885, when he was appointed Postmaster of Lynchburg by President Cleveland, and retired from the paper in order to assume his new duties. His successor was L. S. Marye, who served the *Virginian* as editor until February, 1887, when Mr. Button, having resigned as Postmaster, resumed the editorial position for one month, and finally severed his connection in the succeeding March, when the paper was purchased by a syndicate of Lynchburg gentlemen, and Alexander McDonald was chosen for the position of editor-in-chief, with W. W. Wysor as his assistant

During its eighty years of vigorous life, the *Virginian* has wielded an appreciable power in State and local politics, and has always been a warm advocate of Lynchburg's truest interests, in whatever form they happened to be presented.

THE LYNCHBURG NEWS

was established on the 15th of January, 1866, by Edward D. Christian, a prominent lawyer of the City, and A. Waddill, a practical and experienced printer. Mr. Waddill subsequently became, and still remains, its sole owner. The first editor of the *News* was Robert E. Withers, afterwards United States Senator from Virginia, and now Consul to Hong Kong, China. John G. Perry was the first City Editor. Congressman Thomas Whitehead was afterwards editor-in-chief of the paper, and was succeeded, in April, 1880, by Alexander McDonald, Carter Glass at the same time taking the place of A. J. De Witt as City Editor. In March, 1887, Carter Glass succeeded Mr. McDonald as editor-in-chief. Mr. A. W. Strange has been the Business Manager of the *News* for twenty years, and to his excellent business capacity the success of the paper is largely due. The *News* is now one of the firmly established institutions of Lynchburg, and one of the best paying newspaper establishments in Virginia. It has a large and constantly increasing circulation of all its editions; especially in the rich Southwest, where its bright, newsy pages are familiar to nearly every home circle. It also circulates largely through Pittsylvania, Franklin, Henry and Patrick Counties, and in the counties immediately contiguous to Lynchburg. Its news facilities are unsurpassed by any paper outside of Richmond, and are being improved every week.

THE LYNCHBURG ADVANCE.

This newspaper was established on the 5th of May, 1880, by

Whiteheads, Murrell & Co., who printed daily, semi-weekly and weekly editions, Capt. Thomas C. Whitehead being its Editor. In May, 1882, was formed a joint stock company which conducted the paper for fifteen months under the business management of Mr. W. C. Carrington. In 1883 the company was reorganized, and Mr. T. Davis Evans succeeded Mr. Carrington as Business Manager.

There was a second reorganization in August, 1885, when Major R. H. Glass succeeded Capt. Whitehead as editor-in-chief and Mr. A. J. De Witt became City Editor, Mr. Evans remaining in charge of the Counting Room and Mr. H. W. Baker assuming the responsible position of Foreman and Assistant Editor. The staff of the paper has remained unchanged since the last mentioned date.

Under its present management the *Advance* has made long and rapid strides in public favor, and is now recognized as among the leading journals of the State. Its subscription list was soon doubled and is still steadily increasing. In politics it is "Democratic at all times and under all circumstances," independent in every sense of external influence, and devoted to the dual purpose of publishing all the news of the day, and of influencing public opinion for the public good.

As a pure, interesting and enterprising sheet, the *Advance* has won its way into the hearts and homes of the people, and there are but few Post Offices in Virginia at which it is a stranger, in one or other of its editions. Its circulation in the adjacent States is also becoming important, and its value as an advertising medium is becoming proportionately enhanced.

Being the only afternoon paper in the City, and having secured perfect telegraphic arrangements, it has become a veritable necessity to this enlightened and progressive community.

THE WEEKLY LABOR RECORD.

This Journal, which is "The official organ of District Assembly No. 193, Knights of Labor," was established in June, 1886, by its present Editor and Proprietor, Mr. J. C. Poston. It is devoted to the interests of Labor, in all its numerous ramifications. It is published every Saturday, and has secured a large circulation and a liberal advertising patronage.

MARSHALL LODGE HOME AND RETREAT, FOR THE SICK AND WOUNDED.

This institution, as its name implies, is a monument to local Masonic benevolence and public spirit. It was opened on April 1st, 1886, by Marshall Lodge No. 39, A. F. and A. M., and is governed by a Board of Managers elected by that Lodge. The Home is situated on the corner of Washington and Church Streets, Diamond Hill, within two squares of the line of street cars, and its site is one of the healthiest and most picturesque in the City. It affords accommodation for twenty patients, and during the first year of its existence (ending April 1st, 1887), over sixty sufferers were taken care of within its walls.

The institution contains four private rooms and four ward rooms. Of the latter, two are in a separate building and are reserved for colored patients. Cots have been endowed by the Ladies' Relief Society, the Ladies' Cot Society, (of St. Pauls Episcopal Church,) and the Little Sisters of Mercy, for the use of indigent sufferers. Moderate charges are made to those patients who are able to pay, and in this manner the running expenses of the institution are partially defrayed. The deficit, whatever that may be, is borne by Marshall Lodge. It is a noble charity, and one that has already conferred inestimable blessing upon the sick and suffering of the community. All the physicians of the City give their services free in all cases received at the Home in which the patients are unable to pay, thus securing even to the poorest the advantage of skilled medical treatment. Many lives have doubtless been saved, and many hearts made glad by the care and attention afforded by the Home, which would otherwise have been beyond their reach.

The present officers and Board of Managers of the Marshall Lodge Home and Retreat are as follows: *President*, J. P. Bell; *Vice-President*, T. D. Davis; *Treasurer*, T. D. Jennings; *Secretary*, Dr. C. E. Busey; *Managers*, J. P. Bell, T. D. Davis, T. D. Jennings, R. T. Aunspaugh, R. T. Craighill, T. M. McCorkle, Dr. A. I. Clark, S. D. Preston and E. N. Eubank. The domestic arrangements of the Home are under the charge of the efficient Matron, Mrs. B. B. Cole, assisted by trained nurses.

THE YOUNG MEN'S CHRISTIAN ASSOCIATION OF LYNCHBURG, VA.

This Association was organized on November 26th, 1882, with twenty-three members. Its life at first was very feeble, but when, in April, 1883, the State Convention met in this City, a deep interest in the organization was awakened, and steps were forthwith taken to insure its increased and permanent usefulness. To this end, the City was thoroughly canvassed for the necessary funds by Messrs. W. H. Wren, of Lynchburg; C. A. Licklider, then Secretary of the Association at Petersburg; and — — McIlhaney, of Staunton. The Association then occupied the rooms over the office of Messrs. R. Pollard & Co., on Eighth Street, but the growing membership soon made it necessary to secure more extensive quarters, and on January 1st, 1885, these were found and rented on the corner of Main and Eighth Streets.

In April, 1886, the City was again canvassed for the purpose of raising money sufficient to build a permanent Home worthy of the Association. The handsome and commodious structure on Church Street, between Eighth and Ninth Streets, an engraving of which is shown on the opposite page, was the result of this canvass, and the citizens may well feel proud of this fine building, which was erected at a cost of about $17,000.

Mr. C. A. Licklider was the first Secretary of this Association. He held the office for six months and was succeeded by Mr. Charles Hammersley. In April, 1884, the last named gentleman retired and the duties of the Secretaryship were discharged by Mr. William Cumming until September 1st, 1885, when he resigned to enter the ministry. Mr. Licklider was then recalled, and is now the efficient and enthusiastic Secretary of the Association, which owes much of its prosperity to his capacity and zeal.

At the organization of the Association Mr. W. H. Wren was elected President. He served for two years, and was succeeded by Mr. W. A. Heffernan. Major Thomas J. Kirkpatrick was the next presiding officer, and was followed by Mr. J. P. Pettyjohn, who still fills the chair.

The present officers of the Association are: President, J. P. Pettyjohn; 1st Vice-President, J. G. Payne; 2nd Vice-President, J. L. Thompson; 3rd Vice-President, William Kinnier; Treasurer, J. B. Johnson; Recording Secretary, Christopher Winfree; General Secretary, C. A. Licklider; Assistant Secretary, Walter M. Williams; Superintendent of Gymnasium, Prof. Wyndham Robertson; Directors: R. T. Aunspaugh, N. C. Manson, Jr., M. H. Payne, F. T. Lee, J. T. Yates and Charles W. Button.

The Reading Room is well supplied with a fine class of daily and weekly newspapers, magazines and other periodicals. It is open to all, whether members of the Association or not, and a hearty welcome is extended to all visitors—especially to strangers in the City. To members alone, and their invited guests, belong the privilege of the parlor, chess room and smoking room, educational classes, gymnasium with instruction, and admission to the monthly entertainments.

The membership has now grown to five hundred and forty-five, and is universally admitted to be of immense benefit not only to the individual members but also to the *morale* of the City generally.

On November 4th, 1886, the building was formally opened, and the occasion was marked by an eloquent and impressive address by the Mayor of the City, Mr. N. C. Mansion, Jr., before a largé and enthusiastic audience, and by Capt. L. L. Marks, of Petersburg.

NEW BUILDING OF THE YOUNG MEN'S CHRISTIAN ASSOCIATION.

MILITARY ORGANIZATIONS.

THE LYNCHBURG HOME GUARD.

This Company was organized on November 8th, 1859, and is the only one still surviving in Lynchburg whose history antedates the war. Its original officers were: *Captain*, Samuel Garland, Jr.; *First Lieutenant*, K. Otey; *Second Lieutenant*, M. N. Moorman; *Third Lieutenant*, John G. Meem, Jr.; *Fourth Lieutenant*, Samuel M. Simpson.

On the 23rd of April, 1861, the Home Guard—101 strong—left Lynchburg, by order of the Governor of Virginia, and were mustered into the service of the State on the following day at Richmond.

The War Record of the Company shows that it was engaged in the following battles, affairs and skirmishes, namely: Bull Run, Va., July 18, 1861; Manassas, Va., July 21, 1861; Drainesville, Va., December 19, 1861; Warrenton Junction, Va., March 12, 1862; Yorktown, Va., April 1862; Williamsburg, Va., May 5, 1862; Seven Pines, Va., May 31, 1862; Frazier's Farm, Va., June 30, 1862; Second Battle of Manassas, Va., August 31, 1862; Boonsboro', Md., September 14, 1862; Sharpsburg, Md., September 17, 1862, Suffolk or White Marsh, Va., April 30, 1863; Gettysburg, Pa., July 3, 1863; Fredericksburg, Va., December 13, 1863; Plymouth, N. C., April 18, 1864; Drury's Bluff, Va., May 16, 1864; Cold Harbour, Va., June 1 to 15, 1864; Clay House, Va., June 16 and 17, 1864; Deep Bottom or Nine Mile Road, Va., ———, Chesterfield Line, Va., Winter of 1864–5; Ford's Depot, Va., March 30, 1865; Dinwiddie Court House, Va., March 31, 1865; Five Forks, Va., April 1, 1865; Sailors Creek, Va., April 6, 1865.

It will be seen by the above that the Home Guard was a *fighting* Company from first to last, and this is still further evidenced by the fact that, including members who joined and recruits who followed after the Company was mustered into service, forty-four of its number were killed or died from wounds, six died in the service of disease, twenty-seven were severely wounded and thirty-three wounded but not seriously.

The Company furnished to the Confederate States Army during the war thirty-four officers, as follows: One Brigadier General, two Colonels, four Majors, thirteen Captains and fourteen Lieutenants.

The present officers of the Lynchburg Home Guard are:

K. Otey, Captain,
E. A. Biggers, 1st Lieutenant,
John H. Moore, 2nd "
Frank C. Scruggs, Junior 2d Lieut.
P. T. Withers, Jr., 1st Sergeant,
J. L. McKinney, 2nd "
Thomas Claytor, 3rd "
John D. Oglesby, 4th Sergeant,
W. N. Turner, 5th (or color) "
W. C. Caldwell, 1st Corporal and Acting Q. M. S.
William J. Seabury, 2nd Corporal,
McC. Wade, 3rd Corporal,
John C. Shearer, 4th Corporal.

THE LYNCHBURG LIGHT ARTILLERY BLUES.

This battery was organized on May 5th, 1877. Its original officers were: *Captain*, Frank T. Lee; *First Lieutenant*, William N. Wellford; *Second Lieutenant*, Mosby H. Payne; *Third Lieutenant*, Wm. H. Dudley.

In 1882 the battery went to Baltimore to take part in the great "Oriole" festival. During the grand procession they acted as escort to "Lord Baltimore" and received two beautiful markers' flags, as first prize for best appearance on parade, presented by the Oriole Committee and a Committee from the 1st Maryland Regiment.

Its present officers are:

Robert D. Yancey, Captain,
Samuel H. Dillon, 1st Lieutenant
Alfred A. Mullan, 2nd "
Thomas E. Craddock, 3rd "
James S. Dudley, 1st Sergeant
J. F. Spencer, 2nd "
W. A. Taylor, 3rd "
F. P. Johnson, 4th Serg't (Guidon)
John A. Davis, Q. M. "
James B. Gregory, 1st Corporal
H. A. Southall, 2nd "
R. L. Poindexter, 3rd "
H. A. Hawkins, 4th "

THE LIGHT ARTILLERY BLUES, JUNIOR,

(FORMERLY THE LYNCHBURG ZOUAVES),

were organized on August 25th, 1884, with J. D. Clark as Captain. In the fall of 1886 they reorganized and became affiliated with the Lynchburg Light Artillery Blues, as a junior battery, which now musters thirty-seven youths between the ages of fifteen and eighteen years. They are thoroughly drilled, and present a handsome and military appearance on parade. The juvenile battery is officered as follows:

Captain—J. D. Clark.
First Lieutenant—M. C. Jameson, Jr.
Second Lieutenant—J. L. Wellford.
Junior Second Lieutenant—C. Owen.
Sergeants—1st, Emerson; 2d, Craighill; 3d, Gilbert; 4th, ———; 5th, Blackford; 6th, Lee.
Corporals—1st, McGehee; 2d, Warwick; 3rd, Jameson.
Drummers—Jameson, Wellford, Blackford, Krise.

THE FITZ LEE TROOP

was organized in April, 1885, as the "Wise Troop," and was virtually a reorganization of the original troop of that name which mustered into the service of the State at the beginning of the Civil War, and was disbanded at its close. The name of the troop was changed last year, as above, in honor of the present Governor of Virginia, the dashing and gallant Cavalry General, Fitzhugh Lee, and by his permission. The original officers of the troop were: *Captain*, B. W. Bocock; *First Lieutenant*, A. S. Payne; *Second Lieutenant*, Joseph B. Page; *Third Lieutenant*, Jacob Shaner. Capt. Bocock resigned after serving a year and was succeeded by Captain Payne who, in turn, resigned on April 3rd, 1887.

The present officers of the Fitz Lee Troop are:

Joseph B. Page, Captain,	C. R. Vest, 5th Sergeant
B. W. Bocock, 1st Lieutenant	A. Hauser, color "
Thomas Smith, 2nd "	H. W. Baker, Q. M. "
W. B. Foster, 1st Sergeant	B. O. Mays, 1st Corporal
H. A. Fisher, 2nd "	R. A. Treavey, 2nd "
J. J. Beavers, 3rd "	L. D. Creasy, 3rd "
J. P. Ackerly, 4th "	T. C. Blackburn, 4th "

CONCLUSION.

The story of Lynchburg's rise and progress might be extended indefinitely, and even then the half of its advantages and attractions remain untold. But it is hoped that those already enumerated will prove sufficient to excite the interest and curiosity of the reader who has had no opportunity as yet of visiting the beautiful "Hill City" or of coming into personal contact with its happy, industrious and thriving inhabitants.

The foregoing sketch is but an outline-drawing at the best; but its object has been to produce a faithful *portrait*, rather than a flattering *picture*, and it is now left to the intelligent and impartial public to decide whether the work shall be awarded the credit of having honestly achieved its purpose, or be consigned as a failure to the pitiful doom of perpetual obscurity. It is frankly admitted that the narrative is sadly deficient in literary merit; but as no claim has been made for it on that score, the fear of adverse criticism has not alloyed the gratefulness of the compiler's task.

The outside world is here informed, on the indisputable authority of facts and figures, of the great natural and acquired superiority of our busy City as a Commercial and Industrial Centre, where capital can always find safe and profitable investment, and where honest labor can at all times command steady and lucrative employment. The citizens of Lynchburg may well feel proud of the continued and marked improvement which their trade has shown in all its branches; and in their name a warm invitation is extended to all who feel prompted to investigate the accuracy of the foregoing statements in person, with the promise of a cordial, old-fashioned Virginia welcome.

CITY GOVERNMENT, 1887.

OFFICERS.

Mayor—N. C. Manson, Jr.
Treasurer—John W. Bransford.
Auditor—Kirk Otey.
Collector of City Taxes—R. T. Lacy.
Commissioner of the Revenue—Charles W. Price.
Commonwealth's Attorney—A. H. Burroughs.
City Attorney—R. G. H. Kean.
Clerk of the Courts—Samuel D. Preston.
City Sergeant—Matt. J. Day.
Chief of Police—J. M. Irwin.
City Engineer—Aug. Forsberg.
Superintendent of Water Works—James Allen.
Register of Water Works—Thomas W. Green.
City Surveyor—L. P. Rodes.
High Constable—L. C. Talbot; *Deputy*—R. W. Faris.
Coroner—Dr. Carter Wade.
Clerk of the Market—T. M. Harwood.
Chief Engineer Fire Department—Alexander Thurman.
Keeper of Almshouse—J. B. McGehee.
Physician to Almshouse—Dr. H. G. Latham.
Physician to the Outside Poor—Dr. W. H. Dulaney.
Police Commissioners—D. C. Guy, S. M. McCorkle and W. L. Moorman.
Board of Health—Drs. T. L. Walker, G. W. Thornhill and A. I. Clark.
Overseers of the Poor—Dr. W. H. Dulaney (President), Clinton De Witt, Richard Matthews, S. W. Younger and N. B. Floyd.
Board of Fire Commissioners—G. W. Smith (President), W. H. Snead and E. C. Hamner.
Superintendent of Public Schools—Edward C. Glass.
Board of School Trustees—R. L. Miller (President), J. T. Taylor, Thomas H. Early, W. A. Miller, Camillus Christian, Jacob H. Franklin, J. B. Winfree, J. L. Thompson and W. B. Snead.

COMMON COUNCIL.

President—John W. Carroll.

Clerk—Carter Glass.

First Ward Councilmen—George M. Jones, James I. Lee, W. F. Mathews, P. A. Krise and John P. Pettyjohn.

Second Ward Councilmen—John W. Carroll, Peter J. Otey, James W. Dickerson, Louis P. Shaner and J. D. Sullivan.

Third Ward Councilmen—John D. Holt, Richard L. Miller, Dr. W. T. Walker, Henry Edwards and Jefferson Anderson.

JUSTICES OF THE PEACE.

First Ward—S. R. Wortham, J. B. Crenshaw, W. B. Freeman and E. W. Jones.

Second Ward—F. D. Johnson and John Kelly. (Two vacancies.)

Third Ward—J. W. Breathed and W. B. Snead. (Two vacancies.)

CITY COURTS.

Corporation Court—Judge, Charles P. Latham; Clerk, Samuel D. Preston.

Circuit Court—Judge, J. D. Horseley; Clerk, Samuel D. Preston.

Police Court—Mayor, N. C. Manson, Jr.; Clerk, P. V. Ford.

UNITED STATES OFFICERS.

COURTS.

(MEET IN MARCH AND SEPTEMBER.)

District Court—Judge, John Paul; Clerk, W. M. Elliott; Deputy Clerk, W. B. Tinsley.

Circuit Court—Judge, Hugh L. Bond; Clerk, W. M. Elliott; Deputy Clerk, W. B. Tinsley.

UNITED STATES POST OFFICE.

Postmaster—T. D. Jennings.

Assistant Postmaster—T. D. Davis.

Stamp Clerk—Robert Strother.

Register Clerk—J. A. Bass.

Money Order Clerk—T. D. Davis.

Delivery Clerk—J. C. Kinnier.

Distributing Clerk—J. D. Murrell, Jr.

Mailing Clerk—J. S. Nicholas.

Superintendent of City Delivery—W. J. Seabury.

UNITED STATES SIGNAL OFFICE.

Sergeant in Charge—T. F. Schley.

UNITED STATES INTERNAL REVENUE OFFICE.

Deputy Collector-in-Charge—J. Risque Hutter.
Deputy Collectors—L. P. Rodes and Charles F. Byrne.
Clerk—N. F. Featherston.
District Deputy—John Whitehead.
Gauger—James McDaniel.

LIST OF PRESIDENTS OF THE COMMON COUNCIL.

[NOTE.—Owing to the loss of the earliest Record Book of the Council, the names of its presiding officers from 1805, when the Town of Lynchburg was first incorporated, to 1811, are not known.]

From 1811 to 1817—William Davis.
" 1817 to 1818—Robert Morris.
" 1818 to 1820—William Norvell.
" 1820 to 1822—William Davis, Jr.
" 1822 to 1832—John Thurman.
" 1832 to 1841—Smithson H. Davis.
" 1841 to 1850—John M. Otey.
" 1850 to 1865—John M. Speed.
From 1865 to 1866—Lorenzo Norvell.
" 1866 to 1868—A. B. Rucker.
" 1868 to 1870—John Boisseau, (military appointee.)
" 1870 to 1871—W. M. Black.
" 1871 to 1872—John Robin McDaniel.
" 1872 to 1887—John W. Carroll.

THE MAYORS OF LYNCHBURG.

As a matter of interest to the reader, the following list of the Chief Magistrates of the City, in the order of their succession, is given:

1806 John Wiatt,
1807 Roderick Taliaferro,
1808 Samuel J. Harrison,
1809 John Lynch, Jr.,
1810 M. Lambert,
1811 John Schoolfield,
1812 James Stewart,
1813 Robert Morris,
1814 Samuel J. Harrison,
1815 James Stewart,
1816 John M. Gordon,
1817 Samuel J. Harrison,
1818 William Morgan,
1819 James Stewart,
1820 John Thurman,
1821 Micajah Davis,
1822 John Hancock,
1823 Thomas A. Holcombe,
1824 Albon McDaniel,
1825 John Victor,
1826 Albon McDaniel,
1827 Christopher Winfree,
1828 Albon McDaniel,
1829 Ammon Hancock,
1830 Elijah Fletcher,
1831 John R. D. Payne,
1832 Elijah Fletcher,
1833 John M. Warwick,
1834 Henry M. Didlake,
1835 Samuel J. Wiatt,
1836 Pleasant Labby,
1837 Ammon Hancock,
1838 Martin W. Davenport,
1839 John R. D. Payne,
1840 Samuel Nowlin,
1841 Ammon Hancock,
1842 Henry M. Didlake,
1843 Edwin Mathews,
1844 David W. Burton,
1845 M. Hart,
1646 Henry M. Didlake,
1847 Daniel J. Warwick,
1848 Henry O. Schoolfield,
1849 Edwin Mathews,
1850 Henry M. Didlake,
1851 William D. Branch,
1869 Albon McDaniel, [military appointee, served previously as Mayor in 1824, 1826 and 1828.]
1870 James M. Cobbs,
1872 George H. Burch,
1876 Samuel A. Bailey,
1880 Samuel G. Wingfield,
1882 A. H. Pettigrew,
1884 N. C. Manson, Jr., the present incumbent.

GUIDE TO THE CHURCHES.

PROTESTANT EPISCOPAL.

St. Paul's—Rev. T. M. Carson, Rector. Corner of Church and Seventh Streets.

Grace Memorial—Rev. J. H. Williams, Rector. Corner of Grace and Sixteenth Streets, Diamond Hill.

Christ—Rev. J. H. Williams, Rector. Cabell Street, Daniel's Hill.

Epiphany—No Rector. Occasional services. Salem Turnpike, near Fair Grounds.

CATHOLIC.

Church of the Holy Cross—Rev. J. J. McGuirk, Priest in charge. Corner of Clay and Seventh Streets.

PRESBYTERIAN.

First—Rev. W. T. Hall, D. D., Pastor. Main Street, between Twelfth and Thirteenth.

Second—Rev. J. M. Rawlings, Pastor. Corner of Church and Ninth Streets.

Third—Rev. James R. Crews, Pastor. Cabell Street, Daniel's Hill.

West End Chapel—Rev. J. M. Rawlings, Pastor. Park Avenue, near Fair Grounds.

METHODIST EPISCOPAL.

Court Street—Rev. P. A. Peterson, Pastor. Corner of Court and Seventh Streets.

Centenary—Rev. H. C. Cheatham, Pastor. Church Street near Eleventh.

Memorial—Rev. John Hannon, D. D., Pastor. Corner of Floyd and Ninth Streets.

Daniel's Hill—Rev. W. A. Langhorne, Pastor. Cabell Street, Daniel's Hill.

Trinity Chapel—Rev. H. C. Cheatham, Pastor. Grace Street, near Presbyterian Cemetery.

METHODIST PROTESTANT.

First—Rev. T. E. Coulbourn, Pastor. Church Street, near Eighth.

City Alms House—Rev. S. J. Liggan, Pastor. Corner of Federal and Hollins Streets. Services on the second Sunday of each month.

BAPTIST.

First—Rev. W. R. L. Smith, D. D., Pastor. Corner of Court and Eleventh Streets.

Second—Rev. R. R. Acree, Pastor. Corner of Floyd and Eleventh Streets.

CONTENTS.

GENERAL SUBJECTS.

ILLUSTRATIONS.

ANNOUNCEMENTS.

ANNOUNCEMENTS—CLASSIFIED.

www.ingramcontent.com/pod-product-compliance
Lightning Source LLC
Chambersburg PA
CBHW020542270326
41927CB00006B/684

* 9 7 8 3 7 4 4 7 3 5 6 4 3 *